ANCIENT GREECE

ANCIENT GREECE

Books in this series include:

ANCIENT GREECE

BY DON NARDO

LUCENT
BOOKS

THOMSON

GALE

San Diego • Detroit • New York • San Francisco • Cleveland • New Haven, Conn. • Waterville, Maine • London • Munich

© 2003 by Lucent Books. Lucent Books is an imprint of The Gale Group, Inc.,
a division of Thomson Learning, Inc.

For more information, contact:
Lucent Books
27500 Drake Rd.
Farmington Hills, MI 48334-3535
Or you can visit our Internet site at www.gale.com

LIBRARY OF CONGRESS CATALOGING-IN-PUBLICATION DATA

Nardo, Don, 1947–
    Ancient Greece / by Don Nardo.
        p. cm. — (The history of weapons and warfare)
Summary: Discusses the weapons used by the ancient Greeks and their different means of
warfare.
Includes bibliographical references and index.
    ISBN 1-59018-004-6
    1. Military art and science—Greece—History to 1500—Juvenile literature. 2. Military
weapons—Greece—History To 1500—Juvenile literature. 3. Greece—History, Military To 146
B.C.—Juvenile literature. [1. Military weapons—Greece—History—to 1500. 2. Military art
and science—Greece—History—to 1500. 3. Greece—History, Military—to 146 B.C.] I. Title. II.
Series.
    U33.N37 2003
    355'.00938—dc21

                        2003004894

Contents

Foreword

The earliest battle about which any detailed information has survived took place in 1274 B.C. at Kadesh, in Syria, when the armies of the Egyptian and Hittite empires clashed. For this reason, modern historians devote a good deal of attention to Kadesh. They know that this battle and the war of which it was a part were not the first fought by the Egyptians and their neighbors. Many other earlier conflicts are mentioned in ancient inscriptions found throughout the Near East and other regions, as from the dawn of recorded history city-states fought one another for political or economic dominance.

Moreover, it is likely that warfare long predated city-states and written records. Some scholars go so far as to suggest that the Cro-Magnons, the direct ancestors of modern humans, wiped out another early human group—the Neanderthals—in a prolonged and fateful conflict in the dim past. Even if this did not happen, it is likely that even the earliest humans engaged in conflicts and battles over territory and other factors. "Warfare is almost as old as man himself," writes renowned military historian John Keegan, "and reaches into the most secret places of the human heart, places where self dissolves rational purpose, where pride reigns, where emotion is paramount, where instinct is king."

Even after humans became "civilized," with cities, writing, and organized religion, the necessity of war was widely accepted. Most people saw it as the most natural means of defending territory, maintaining security, or settling disputes. A character in a dialogue by the fourth-century B.C. Greek thinker Plato declares:

> All men are always at war with one another. . . . For what men in general term peace is only a name; in reality, every city is in a natural state of war with every other, not indeed proclaimed by heralds, but everlasting. . . . No possessions or institutions are of any value to him who is defeated in battle; for all the good things of the conquered pass into the hands of the conquerors.

Considering the thousands of conflicts that have raged across the world since Plato's time, it would seem that war is an inevitable part of the human condition.

War not only remains an ever-present reality, it has also had undeniably crucial and far-reaching effects on human society and its development. As Keegan puts it, "History lessons remind us that the states in which we live . . . have come to us through conflict, often of the most bloodthirsty sort." Indeed, the world's first and oldest nation-state,

Egypt, was born out of a war between the two kingdoms that originally occupied the area; the modern nations of Europe rose from the wreckage of the sweeping barbarian invasions that destroyed the Roman Empire; and the United States was established by a bloody revolution between British colonists and their mother country.

Victory in these and other wars resulted from varying factors. Sometimes the side that possessed overwhelming numbers or the most persistence won; other times superior generalship and strategy played key roles. In many cases, the side with the most advanced and deadly weapons was victorious. In fact, the invention of increasingly lethal and devastating tools of war has largely driven the evolution of warfare, stimulating the development of new counter-weapons, strategies, and battlefield tactics. Among the major advances in ancient times were the composite bow, the war chariot, and the stone castle. Another was the Greek phalanx, a mass of close-packed spearmen marching forward as a unit, devastating all before it. In medieval times, the stirrup made it easier for a rider to stay on his horse, increasing the effectiveness of cavalry charges. And a progression of late medieval and modern weapons—including cannons, handguns, rifles, submarines, airplanes, missiles, and the atomic bomb—made warfare deadlier than ever.

Each such technical advance made war more devastating and therefore more feared. And to some degree, people are drawn to and fascinated by what they fear, which accounts for the high level of interest in studies of warfare and the weapons used to wage it. Military historian John Hackett writes:

An inevitable result of the convergence of two tendencies, fear of war and interest in the past, has seen a thirst for more information about the making of war in earlier times, not only in terms of tools, techniques, and methods used in warfare, but also of the people by whom wars are and have been fought and how men have set about the business of preparing for and fighting them.

These themes—the evolution of warfare and weapons and how it has affected various human societies—lie at the core of the books in Lucent's History of Weapons and Warfare series. Each book examines the warfare of a pivotal people or era in detail, exploring the beliefs about and motivations for war at the time, as well as specifics about weapons, strategies, battle formations, infantry, cavalry, sieges, naval tactics, and the lives and experiences of both military leaders and ordinary soldiers. Where possible, descriptions of actual campaigns and battles are provided to illustrate how these various factors came together and decided the fate of a city, a nation, or a people. Frequent quotations by contemporary participants or observers, as well as by noted modern military historians, add depth and authenticity. Each volume features an extensive annotated bibliography to guide those readers interested in further research to the most important and comprehensive works on warfare in the period in question. The series provides students and general readers with a useful means of understanding what is regrettably one of the driving forces of human history—violent human conflict.

The Greek Way of War and Its Legacy in the West

Sometimes for the better, but more often for the worse, war was an incessant and accepted feature of ancient Greek life. "What men in general term peace," wrote the Athenian philosopher Plato in the fourth century B.C., "is only a name. In reality, every city is in a natural state of war with every other, not indeed proclaimed by the heralds, but everlasting."[1] With these rather pessimistic but accurate words, Plato recognized the fact that the Greeks almost relentlessly squabbled among themselves, as well as fought foreign peoples when the need and opportunity arose.

Frequent fighting among the Greek cities was partly attributable to the fact that Greece was never a unified country in ancient times. Mainland Greece and various neighboring Aegean and Mediterranean islands and coasts were divided into numerous independent city-states (and sometimes kingdoms). Each viewed itself as a separate nation and staunchly protected its territory and way of life. In fact, it was principally the very inability of these states to unite into a strong nation that brought about their eventual downfall.

What is more, in their frequent eagerness to kill one another, the Greeks established modes of and attitudes about warfare that long outlived them. The Romans, who eventually conquered and long ruled the Greek lands, absorbed many of these military ideas. And they, in their turn, passed them along to later European and European-based peoples. Indeed, the worldwide success of Western civilization from Greco-Roman times to the present, made possible by the waging and winning of wars too numerous to list and too brutal to contemplate, owes an incalculable debt to the Greeks. As noted military historian Victor D. Hanson puts it:

> The Greeks created a unique approach to organized fighting that . . . proved to be the most lethal brand of warfare in the Mediterranean, the

chief tenets of which have characterized Western military tradition ever since. . . . Western warfare is terrifying—both relatively and absolutely. The march of European armies has been both reckless and murderous, ultimately smashing anything that has raised its head in over two millennia of organized military opposition.[2]

Superiority of Arms and Discipline

The tremendous effectiveness and success of Western warfare over the span of the last two millennia, says Hanson, can be traced to "a series of practices created at the beginning of Western culture by the Greeks."[3] Among these military customs and beliefs that were at one time uniquely Greek is advanced technology. For over five centuries, Greek weapons and armor proved consistently superior in design and craftsmanship to those of non-Greeks. Time after time, this advantage enabled Greek armies to smash and terrify much larger armies of Persians and other opponents; and in similar fashion, later Western societies managed to maintain or develop arms systems on the technological cutting edge and used them to defeat and demoralize their enemies.

Other aspects of Greek warfare made it unique and highly successful in its heyday,

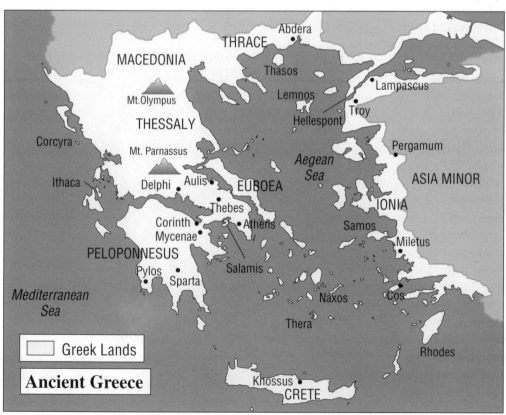

as well as a model for later effective military systems. Greek troops were usually highly disciplined on the battlefield. Also, they were often members of democratic assemblies that helped decide whether to fight, and if so where and when. As a rule, they chose to resolve said fighting quickly, in one or a few major, decisive encounters. They also relied most heavily on the muscular strength of infantry (foot soldiers), rather than on cavalry (horsemen) or missile throwers (archers, slingers, and so forth). And to this day, infantry remains the backbone of Western armies. In addition, the Greeks readily borrowed the military ideas of other peoples. Says Hanson, "No Greek felt ashamed or unsure about adopting, modifying, rejecting—or im-

proving—military practices that were originally not his own."[4]

"Mass Duels and the Morality" of War

Some of these flexible and decisive qualities of Greek armies might be canceled out, or at least blunted, when Greeks fought other Greeks. Indeed, a kind of ritualized, honor-driven style of fighting developed within Greece itself beginning in the eighth or seventh century B.C. The "manly" approach was for foot soldier to meet foot soldier face-to-face, with only the weapons and armor each could carry, along with his individual strength and courage, to decide the outcome. Usually, the two sides agreed to meet in massed in-

Greek foot soldiers easily repel an attack of enemy cavalry. Greek influence meant that infantry became the backbone of Western armies.

fantry formations (phalanxes) on open, flat ground where no one could hide or stage an ambush. Such a battle, remarks noted historian F.E. Adcock, was "a 'mass duel,' a trial of strength; and the verdict of the trial was accepted. . . . Through armistice and negotiations, a peace was often reached."[5]

Whether utilized for struggles against non-Greeks or fellow Greeks, Greek warfare was rarely static in character; rather, it underwent bursts of change as well as an overall evolution. Unfortunately for the Greeks, however, the Romans ultimately proved to be more innovative and flexible. The Romans eventually recognized the few flaws in the Greek system and wisely instituted changes in weaponry and tactics that exploited the Greek weaknesses. Ever since that time, Western societies have strived for and achieved new advances in military science. And they have increasingly refined the art of killing, following the example the Greeks set long ago.

At the same time, the West still finds itself in a moral dilemma it inherited from the Greeks. Despite the quality of their arms and armor and tendency to employ them often, the Greeks frequently questioned the legality and ethics of war. In their minds, war had to be morally justified. Sometimes the justification seemed obvious, as when outsiders attacked, forcing the Greeks to fight for their very survival.

Other times, fighting was motivated by petty jealousies and political disagreements among Greek states. As free men, Greeks everywhere often debated whether such reasons justified the potential risks of losing—including humiliation and dishonor, as well as loss of life and territory. That same debate continues today each time a Western nation considers going to war. Indeed, this fundamental problem of warfare raised long ago by the Greeks has yet to be resolved in a world dominated by their political and military descendants.

CHAPTER ONE

Bronze Swords and Charging Chariots: Early Greek Warfare

The story of ancient Greek warfare, like that of the Greeks themselves, begins in the distant past with the rise of the Minoans and Mycenaeans. The Minoans (named by modern scholars after a mythical king, Minos) were a highly civilized people who inhabited Crete and a few other southern Aegean Islands. Although they did not speak Greek, they created the first advanced civilization on Greek soil and came to exert a powerful cultural and probably also military influence on the Mycenaeans. The latter (named for their imposing fortress at Mycenae, in southeastern Greece) were the area's first Greek-speakers. They settled the Greek mainland sometime in the early second millennium B.C.

These early peoples prospered in the Bronze Age (ca. 3000–1100 B.C.), so named because they fashioned their tools and weapons from bronze, an alloy of copper and tin. Near the start of the late Bronze Age (ca. 1500–1100 B.C.), the mainland Mycenaeans organized themselves into several small but powerful and aggressive kingdoms. Sometime in the 1400s B.C., one or more of these realms invaded Crete and took over the Minoan palaces. Mycenaean warlords then controlled the Aegean sphere for the next two centuries, each ruling from one of several mighty stone palace-fortresses, like the one at Mycenae, that had risen on the mainland. Indeed, the Mycenaeans "were spectacular builders," wrote the late, noted historian C.M. Bowra. "Their palaces were built within formidable citadels with walls 10 feet thick, and some of their royal tombs were enormous beehive structures made of stones weighing, sometimes, as much as 120 tons."[6]

The immensity of these fortifications offers a clue to the nature of Bronze Age Greek warfare, about which scholars still know relatively little. It remains unclear how often and on what scale the Mycenaean kingdoms fought one another, for instance. But the fact that they heavily fortified their palace-centers suggests that attacks and sieges were not rare occurrences. Among the other clues indicating that the Mycenaeans were warlike: The graves of their aristocrats were usually filled with weapons; and their surviving paintings often depict armor-clad warriors bearing weapons.

The Use of War Chariots

Unfortunately, a few badly ruined fortresses and some scattered remnants of weapons, armor, and paintings are the only material artifacts scholars have for the difficult task of reconstructing Bronze Age Greek warfare. No written descriptions of soldiers and battles, if any ever existed, have survived from that period. Still, even the small amount of evidence available has allowed scholars to piece together an intriguing, if incomplete, picture of Mycenaean weapons and battle tactics.

First, Mycenaean paintings and palace inventory lists frequently depict or mention chariots. The question is how the Bronze Age Greeks used them. Did they consist merely of a few "prestige vehicles" that ferried leaders to the battlefield, where they dismounted and fought on foot? Or were chariots used in greater

Modern tourists survey the lower section of the massive stones of the ruins at Mycenae. The Plain of Argos is visible in the distance.

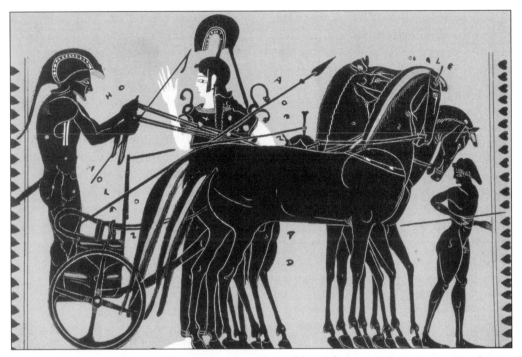

This painting from a later Greek vase, depicting the goddess Athena assisting a young warrior, shows a chariot similar to those used in Mycenaean times.

numbers as actual offensive weapons in combat? Military historian Peter Connolly points out that inventories from the palace of Knossus (in northern Crete) list some 340 chariot frames and a thousand chariot wheels. This, he says, suggests a very heavy use of vehicles that were extremely expensive to build and maintain. The only credible way the builders could have gotten their money's worth was to center their warfare around these mobile units. Indeed, Connolly writes: "These can hardly have been used just to get the nobility to the front line. The ratio of three sets of wheels to each body implies that they were intended for rougher service than this. They must have been used for fighting."[7]

This view is supported by what scholars know about chariot warfare in neighboring lands in the era in question. During the middle of the second millennium B.C., when the Mycenaean kingdoms were rising, the Egyptians, Assyrians, Hittites, and other ancient Near Eastern peoples developed battlefield tactics in which masses of chariots carrying archers charged one another. The culmination of this mode of fighting was the great battle at Kadesh (or Qadesh, in southern Syria), fought around 1285 B.C. between the Egyptians and Hittites. Thousands of chariots took part, while specially trained foot soldiers followed, supported, and mopped up after the charioteers and archers. The Mycenaeans had frequent contact with and were strongly influenced by the Near East in this period. So they likely used at least a modified form of such warfare. Although Greece has few flat plains large enough to contain massed chariot charges, smaller versions, involving several dozen and perhaps occasionally a few hundred chariots, were certainly viable.

Islands in a Sea of Arrows

In fact, used together, the chariot and composite bow (made of wood and horn, which gave the weapon more power and range), appear to have been the major offensive weapons in late Bronze Age Greek land warfare. Vanderbilt University scholar Robert Drews provides this plausible reconstruction of a chariot battle of the period:

[The] opposing chariot forces would hurtle towards each other . . . the squadrons maintaining an assigned order and the archers beginning to discharge their arrows as soon as the enemy came within range (perhaps at a distance of two hundred meters [660 feet] or more). The archers must have shot ever more rapidly and vigorously as the opposing forces closed the distance between them. Of course, many horses were killed or wounded. The whole point of the battle . . . was to bring down as many of the opponent's chariots as possible. . . . After the surviving teams had made their way past each other, the archers may have faced the rear of their vehicles and fired

---

FIGURE-EIGHT AND TOWER SHIELDS

Cambridge University scholar A.M. Snodgrass, a noted authority on Greek weapons and fighting, describes Mycenaean shields in this excerpt from Arms and Armour of the Greeks. *It is clear from their design that they were made to protect soldiers from rains of arrows.*

There are two types of shield represented on the monuments of this period, and both very large—four feet or more in height. . . . They can only have been made of ox-hide, and indeed are sometimes shown dappled in black and white, but there are also occasional hints of metal reinforcement. The commoner of the two varieties is in the shape of a rough figure-of-eight when seen from the back or front; in profile

it is seen to be of strongly convex [curved] form, with a "waist," slightly pinched in, rather less than half way down. . . . Less common and slightly smaller is the plain "tower" shield, which had straight rims at the sides but an upward curve in the top edge and, again, a strong lateral convexity which shows in profile views. Both shields . . . gave some protection to the warrior's sides as well as his front. But they must have been extremely unwieldy; there is no sign that they had handles. . . . It is remarkable that body-shields of this size are occasionally mentioned in the Iliad; in particular, the shield "like a tower" which [the Greek warrior] Ajax regularly uses is surely to be identified with this second type of body-shield.

once or twice at their opponents as they receded. Then the two forces, if they were still cohesive, must have wheeled around and begun their second charge, this time from the opposite direction.[8]

Meanwhile, groups of "runners"—foot soldiers armed with swords, spears, or both—followed alongside the chariots.

Their tasks were to clear the field of capsized chariots, capture or kill fallen enemy archers, and rescue their own fallen bowmen and charioteers. Whenever possible, the runners would have placed themselves behind the chariots, tiny islands of protection in a chaotic sea of flying arrows.

The danger posed by such rains of arrows naturally raises the question of how

ARMOR FOR A BRONZE AGE KNIGHT

In this excerpt from his colorful book The Greek Armies, *ancient military historian Peter Connolly describes the Dendra armor, which was likely worn by a chariot crewman.*

In 1960, at Dendra, not far from Mycenae, a late 15th century B.C. warrior's grave was discovered. This grave contained a complete suit of armor. This very complex armor consists of two main pieces for the chest and back. These are joined on the left side by a primitive hinge. There is a bronze loop on the right side of the front plate and a similar loop on each shoulder. These fitted into slots in the back plate to join the right side and shoulders. Large shoulder guards fitted over the cuirass [chest protector]. There were also arm guards and a deep neck guard. Three pairs of curved plates hung from

the waist to protect the thighs. All these pieces were made of beaten bronze lined with leather which was turned over the edges of the bronze. Two triangular plates were found lying on the chest. These were attached to the shoulder guards and gave added protection to the chest.

Modern depictions of Homeric warriors usually show them bearing spears and short swords as these early hoplites are outfitted.

These Bronze Age Greek sword blades are now missing their handles. Most swords of the period were designed for thrusting.

the chariot crewmen protected themselves. It stands to reason that they must have had some kind of defensive armor. And in fact, sculptures and paintings from ancient Egypt, Cyprus, and elsewhere from this period show armored outfits made of copper or bronze scales sewn or glued to leather or linen jerkins. Attached to the top was a metal tube that protected the neck, chin, and mouth. Even more impressive is a massive suit of bronze armor (not unlike that of a medieval knight) discovered in 1960 at Dendra, near Mycenae. Such armor was much too expensive

A detail from the so-called Warrior Vase, dating from about 1200–1150 B.C., shows soldiers who might have entered Greece from eastern Europe.

for use by average soldiers and must have been worn by a few elite fighters. Also, the Dendra armor was far too heavy and inflexible for a foot soldier, whereas it would have been very practical as protection against a rain of arrows for a man standing on a chariot.

By contrast, foot soldiers in Bronze Age Greece apparently wore little or no armor, except perhaps toward the very end of the era. Besides aiding aristocratic chariot archers in battle, ordinary soldiers no doubt had other important tasks. They likely attacked and tried to scale the walls of the citadels and conversely defended the battlements against such attackers, guarded the camps where the chariots stopped while on the march, and pursued enemies in rough terrain where chariots could not maneuver.

The bronze swords such soldiers wielded were of many types. A number of early Mycenaean swords had long, thin blades; such weapons were designed for thrusting, not cutting, and they may have been used mainly for fighting duels. By the late fourteenth century B.C., shorter swords designed for chopping or hacking, as well as various daggers, were widely used. Evidence suggests that these remained secondary weapons; a soldier probably used his sword only when he lost or broke his spear.

The Curtain Closes on Bronze Age Warfare

Toward the end of the Mycenaean period, however, a new, very formidable kind of sword appeared in mainland Greece. A

In the Dark Age, chariots similar to this one became mainly prestige vehicles to ferry prominent warriors to and from the battlefield.

long slashing weapon that could take off a person's arm in a single blow, it proved to be the precursor of the very successful iron offensive sword utilized for centuries by the later Greeks and Romans. This new sword was developed by tribesmen from central and eastern Europe (perhaps originally in what is now Hungary).

Moreover, this development seems to have coincided with the appearance of well-armored foot soldiers in southern Greece. A row of such troops can be seen marching in a painting on the so-called Warrior Vase, discovered at Mycenae. They wear long-sleeved jerkins (some covered with body armor), greaves (lower-leg protectors), horned helmets with upright crests, and carry crescent-shaped shields.

The origins and significance of these new soldiers remain controversial. First, the crescent-shaped shields and several other military elements depicted on the Warrior Vase are not typically Mycenaean, but quite characteristic of central and eastern Europe, like the swords. Some scholars believe that the soldiers depicted on the vase are in fact not Mycenaeans, but instead mercenaries (hired troops) recruited from tribes living north of the Mycenaean sphere to aid one or more Mycenaean warlords.

The weapons and fighting style of these mercenaries may well have helped bring about the downfall of the Mycenaean kingdoms. In one intriguing scenario suggested by Professor Drews, among others, these hired soldiers were highly impressed by the vast caches of gold and other valuables accumulated by the Mycenaean kings. More importantly, the newcomers quickly realized that their own weaponry and fighting

methods were more than a match for those of the people who had hired them. Soldiers returning home spread the word; before long, large invasion forces descended on the palace-centers of southern Greece, and these armies rendered the chariot corps obsolete. According to Drews:

> By the beginning of the twelfth century [B.C.] . . . the size of a king's chariotry ceased to make much difference, because by that time chariotry everywhere had become vulnerable to a new kind of infantry. [Such] infantries . . . used weapons and guerilla tactics that were characteristic of barbarian hill people but had never been tried en masse in the plains and against the centers of the late Bronze Age kingdoms. . . . A long slashing sword had been available in temperate Europe for centuries, and javelins [throwing spears] everywhere for millennia. Until shortly before 1200 B.C., however, it had never occurred to anyone that infantrymen with such weapons could outmatch chariots.[9]

In this compelling scenario, hordes of these well-armed and armored northern infantrymen easily defeated the numerically fewer and militarily less formidable runners and other Mycenaean foot soldiers. Then they swarmed the chariots, dispatching horses, drivers, and archers alike with javelins and slashing swords. The slaughter left the Mycenaean citadels and their treasures open to plunder and closed the curtain on the first age of Greek warfare.

ACHILLES AND HECTOR
FIGHT TO THE DEATH

The fight between the Greek warrior Achilles and the Trojan champion Hector in book 22 of Homer's *Iliad* is one of the highlights of that epic poem. As the two men come together in mortal combat, Achilles hurls his spear but misses. Then Hector throws his own spear, which hits his opponent's shield dead center but glances off. Cursing, Hector draws his sword and, in Homer's words, swoops "like a soaring eagle launching down from the dark clouds to earth to snatch some helpless lamb." Achilles, who has recovered his spear, charges, too, and searches for an opening somewhere on Hector's body. Finally, Hector's throat is momentarily exposed and, as Homer tells it:

"There, as Hector charged in fury, brilliant Achilles drove his spear and the point went stabbing clean through the tender neck; but the heavy bronze weapon failed to slash the windpipe—Hector could still gasp out some words, some last reply. . . . At the point of death, Hector, his helmet flashing, said, 'I know you well—I see my fate before me. . . . But now beware, or my curse will draw gods' wrath upon your head, that day when Paris and lord Apollo—for all your fighting heart—destroy you at the Scaean Gates!' Death cut him short. The end closed in around him. Flying free of his limbs, his soul went winging down to the House of Death."

Achilles, with his war chariot, drags the body of the slain Hector around the walls of Troy.

"Heroes" of the Dark Age

This theory conforms quite well to the archaeological evidence relating to the end of the Greek Bronze Age. Scholars have long known that the Aegean sphere, as well as many parts of the Near East, underwent a period of unexpected and unprecedented upheaval between 1200 and 1100 B.C. Most of the major Mycenaean strongholds were sacked and burned, never to be rebuilt. Writing, record keeping, large-scale political organization, and other aspects of advanced civilization all but vanished. And Greece slipped into what is now referred to as its Dark Age (ca. 1110–ca. 800 B.C.), a period about which scholars know very little. In the Dark Age, the Minoan-Mycenaean world steadily passed into legend, and the surviving Greeks (including any invaders who had recently settled the area) more or less forgot their heritage. Poverty was widespread. And most people lived in small villages and began identifying themselves only with the particular isolated valley or island where they lived.

People in these small, isolated communities still fought with their neighbors, so warfare remained a very real part of life. But the nature of warfare had changed considerably. As in the case of the Bronze Age, physical evidence of warfare in the Dark Age is scattered and meager. Fortunately, though, two extremely important later written sources do cast some rays of light on Dark Age fighting. These are the *Iliad* and the *Odyssey,* epic poems attributed to the legendary eighth-century B.C. bard Homer. The centerpiece of these works is the famous Trojan War, in which the Greeks sacked Troy, a prosperous city on the northwestern coast of Asia Minor (what is now Turkey).

Scholars now know that the Greeks in Homer's poems were actually Mycenaeans. Shortly before the fall of their kingdoms, some Mycenaean warlords may have attacked and burned Troy. The memory of that event survived the collapse of Bronze Age culture and was later preserved in oral traditions fondly recalling an era that later Greeks called the "Age of Heroes." These stories then passed along from one generation to the next by word of mouth. And they became the basis for the epic poems that reached their pinnacle several hundred years later under Homer.

Various episodes and descriptions in Homer's *Iliad* suggest that Dark Age warfare, like society itself in that era, was for a long time smaller scale and less organized. First, the chariot was no longer a major offensive device. For the Homeric warriors, chariots are mainly prestige vehicles that taxi leading warriors to the battlefield. Once there, the fighters dismount and fight hand-to-hand, often squaring off one-on-one in heroic displays of single combat.

Some archaeological evidence supports this hero-centered picture of warfare in which principal warriors were perhaps the chiefs or chosen champions of individual villages or districts. The Dark Age battlefield, classical scholar John Lazenby writes, was

dominated by a few, comparatively well-armed, aristocratic "heroes." The main weapon seems to have been the throwing-spear, and such a weapon perhaps limits the extent to which [military] tactics can begin to be refined, and leads to the glorification of individual exploits we find in Homer.[10]

This reliance on the throwing spear, backed up by a slashing sword, is exactly what one would expect from fighters descended from the infantrymen who had used such weapons to swarm and destroy the Bronze Age chariots. Such weapons and tactics also closely match those described by Homer. The Greek and Trojan champions of the *Iliad* each carry two or more spears into battle; and they usually begin their one-on-one encounters at a distance, with well-aimed javelin throws. In the famous climactic fight between Achilles and Hector, for example, the men first heave their spears and miss. Only then does Hector draw his sword and move in on his opponent. Meanwhile, Achilles manages to retrieve his spear and plunges it into Hector's neck, killing him.

On the Threshold of a New Age

Such single combats between champions were not the only aspect of battle Homer described. Larger, more formal formations of foot soldiers, armed with spears and swords like their leaders, also play a key role in the *Iliad*. The reason for this mixture of fighting styles is that Homer's descriptions of warfare combine aspects of Dark Age fighting with aspects from his own era. Homer lived in the early stages of what modern scholars call the Archaic Age (ca. 800–500 B.C.). During these years Greece recovered from its cen-

turies of decline, and new political-social units commonly described as city-states rose. The new kind of warfare engaged in by the city-states centered around heavily armored infantrymen, called hoplites, who fought in large battlefield formations known as phalanxes. Homer's works, especially the *Iliad,* contain numerous references to such fighting. As Professor Hanson puts it, these epic poems

are probably a rough portrait of Greece between 750 and 680 [B.C.], and thus give our first glimpse of war at the very end of the Dark Age. . . . The core of Homeric society is largely a world of assemblies, councils, colonization, mass fighting, and intensive agriculture, in which comrades struggle for their own fatherland—a poetic cosmos that is still recognizable as the early city-state. The poet has inherited a very old story with plot, characters, and a few archaic details, but the material and literary contents of the poem are mostly from his own time and place.[11]

Indeed, Homer lived on the threshold of a new age of warfare, the effectiveness and fateful results of which he could never have foreseen. The hoplite revolution was about to produce a warrior of skill and sheer lethality far beyond any seen before in the world. The *Iliad* marks more than the beginning of Western literature, therefore; it also contains a small but important echo of the birth of the unique fighter who would make the spectacular triumph of Europe and Western civilization possible.

CHAPTER TWO

Farmers in Armor: The Development of the Hoplite Phalanx

The emergence of hoplite warfare coincided with and indeed developed in response to the rise of city-states and citizen militias across Greece. To understand this military revolution, therefore, one must first grasp the sweeping changes that occurred with the rise of city-states and the citizen-farmers who constituted their backbone.

Many of Greece's Dark Age villages slowly but steadily grew into large, increasingly prosperous towns. And each such town came to dominate the military and cultural affairs of a valley, island, or other local region. These city-states that emerged in the early Archaic Age thought of themselves as tiny independent nations and were very territorial, that is, protective of their local land holdings. Beyond a city's central town stretched a few dozen (in a few cases, several hundred) square miles of farmland, punctuated here and there by small villages. Much of this land had remained wild and uncultivated in the early Dark Age; but over time a new class of hardy, independent farmers reclaimed

the countryside, which became intensively cultivated with grapevines, olive trees, grains, and other crops.

Meanwhile, profound political changes were under way. Rule by powerful chiefs and aristocrats eventually began to give way to more democratic councils and assemblies of citizens. This happened in large part because the tough, independent farmers came to make up a major portion of the citizenry; and they neither needed nor wanted control by aristocratic or other ruling elites.

Moreover, these citizen-farmers became not only the economic backbone of the typical city-state, but also the source of its military strength. To protect their holdings from farmers in rival states, they formed citizen militias that from time to time took up arms and settled border disputes in short but violent and decisive military encounters. Victor Hanson explains that the members of these local militias—full-time farmers and part-time but highly effective fighters—"helped to establish agrarian control [i.e., control by the farmers] of the political life of their respective city-states."[12] Thus, he continues, "the practice of Greek warfare [was] made anew." It represented

> a revolutionary shift in the nature of conflict and society, the first emergence in European culture, or in any other culture, of a large group of middling [middle-class] landowners who craft a military agenda to reflect their own agrarian needs [i.e., the need to protect their land and crops from destruction].[13]

The Hoplite's Shield

By the late eighth century B.C., that agrarian agenda had produced well-organized military units and tactics built around hoplites—heavily armored infantry soldiers. These fighters dominated warfare in Greece and the rest of the Mediterranean sphere for the remainder of the Archaic Age and throughout the Classical Age (ca. 500–323 B.C.) that followed. The term *hoplite* may derive from the Greek word *hopla,* meaning "heavy equipment." "Heavy" is certainly appropriate in describing a hoplite, for his bronze body armor and shield of wood and bronze often weighed forty to

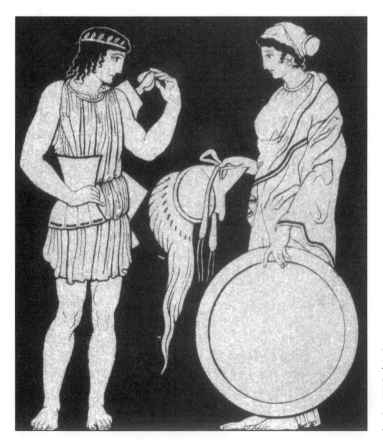

In this vase painting, a young hoplite fastens his cuirass (in this case a linothorax), *while his wife holds his helmet and shield.*

fifty pounds or more. He also wielded a thrusting spear with an iron tip and a short iron-bladed slashing sword. For this reason, hoplites were designated as "heavy infantry," a common term in Western warfare ever since.

This extensive and very heavy array of arms and armor carried by a hoplite was called his panoply. The most basic element of the panoply was the shield, or *hoplon* (also *aspis*). The average *hoplon* was about three feet in diameter and weighed roughly seventeen to eighteen pounds. It was gently concave (curved inward) with a wooden core reinforced on the outside by a coating of bronze (although sometimes by layers of ox hide).

The inside of such a shield was lined with leather and featured a distinctive gripping system. This consisted of a bronze strip with a loop, the *porpax,* in the middle, through which the hoplite passed his left forearm; and a leather handle, the *antilabe,* which he grasped with his left hand. (Without the *porpax,* the shield was largely useless because it was too heavy to hold upright with the hand alone. For this reason, when the soldiers of Sparta—the

This modern depiction shows all the major elements of a hoplite's panoply, including cuirass, helmet, greaves, shield, spear, and sword.

leading land power in Greece in the Classical Age—returned home from battle, each removed the *porpax* from his shield; that way the Spartan serfs, called helots, could not utilize the shields in a rebellion.) Because the hoplite's shield rested on his arm, he could let go of the *antilabe* and hold a spare weapon in his left hand without losing his shield. This ingenious gripping system also helped to relieve the burden of the shield's considerable weight.

Just how much of a burden *was* a hoplite's shield, along with his other battle gear, when he had to exert himself? Attempting to answer this question, in 1973 a group of professors at Pennsylvania State University conducted a unique experiment. They chose ten young physical education majors in top physical condition and attached fifteen pounds of weights to each. Each was also given a nine-pound simulated shield and instructed to hold it upright with his left arm. The young men then began running, as if charging an enemy formation. Not one was able to keep the shield chest-high for more than seventy-five yards, and most were unable to run farther than three hundred yards. One, a varsity long-distance runner, managed to run a mile, but collapsed in a state of total exhaustion. The burdens these students carried were considerably lighter than an ancient hoplite's total panoply.[14] This underscores the difficulty hoplites must have faced trying to fight in full armor and explains why their battles tended to be quick, contained, and decisive.

Hoplite shields were ornamented, sometimes highly so. Ancient vase paintings show that sometimes a leather curtain hung down from the shield's bottom rim. This probably began as a feature to protect the soldier's legs against arrows and other missiles; but over time it may have taken on a more decorative function. On occasion, soldiers decorated the inside surfaces of their shields, a practice apparently popular in Boeotia (the region dominated by Thebes, lying to the north of the Athenian-controlled territory of Attica).

More often, however, the outer surfaces of the shields bore decorations, usually referred to as shield "devices." Some were designed to inspire fear in the enemy; others to indicate family background or military rank; and still others to denote nationality (i.e., one's city-state). A famous example of the latter was the letter *L* on the shields of Spartan hoplites (standing for Lakedaimon, the traditional ancient name for Sparta). Similarly, hoplites from Thebes pictured a club (belonging to their patron, the semidivine hero Heracles); Mantinea, a trident (symbol of their patron, the sea god Poseidon); Athens, an *A;* Sicyonia, an *S;* Tegea, a *T;* and the island of Rhodes, a rose.

Other Elements of the Panoply

After his shield, a hoplite's second line of defense was a breastplate called a cuirass, which protected his torso. According to John Warry, an authority on ancient warfare:

The most expensive type was the muscled cuirass made of bronze, but the most common type of protection was a cuirass made up of numerous

THE AWFUL SOUNDS OF HOPLITE BATTLE

In this excerpt from The Western Way of War, *his classic study of hoplite warfare, noted scholar Victor D. Hanson provides this evocative description of the awful sounds of battle. These must have haunted the participants, for several ancient writers mentioned them.*

The entire noise of men and equipment was concentrated onto the small area of the ancient battlefield—itself usually a small plain encircled by mountains, which only improved the acoustics [magnified the sounds]. . . . The *nature* of the sound also changed from that of recognizable human speech—the war cry or song . . . to a terrible cacophony [din] of smashed bronze, wood, and flesh. . . . The Greeks recognized that the peculiar noise of this initial crash came from a variety of sources. First, there was the dull thud of bronze against wood as either the metal spear point made its way through the wood core of a hoplite shield, or as soldiers struck their shields against the bronze breastplates and helmets of the enemy, or as wooden shield was bashed into shield. . . . The live sounds were more animal-like than human: the concerted groans of men exerting themselves, pushing forward in group effort with their bodies and shields against the immovable armor of the enemy. . . . Finally . . . there were all too often the noises of human misery. Here arose a tortured symphony of shrieks as a man went down with a wound to the groin, the steady sobbing of a soldier in extremis [dying], a final gasp of fright as the spear thrust found its way.

The noise of battle rings out as Greek hoplites mow down an enemy force.

layers of linen or canvas glued together to form a stiff shirt (*linothorax*). These were often reinforced with metal plates or scales. This [largely] replaced the earlier bronze bell type [by the late sixth century B.C.]. The cuirass itself consisted of a body piece with arm holes cut out and the bottom cut into two layers of "feathers" (*pteruges*). This wrapped around the body and was laced together on the left-hand side, where the join was protected by the shield. A yoke which bent down over the shoulders and tied to the chest completed the cuirass.[15]

The panoply had other protective features, including a bronze helmet. The most popular type of helmet in the late Archaic Age and on into the Classic Age was the "Corinthian," which was beaten out of a single sheet of bronze. It had eye-slits and breathing spaces for the nose and mouth. There were many variations, some with cutouts for the ears (since it was otherwise difficult to hear when wearing a helmet), some with movable visors or cheek pieces, and others topped by decorative plumes of horsehair. No evidence for padded linings has been found. Instead, the wearer apparently either wore a close-fitting cap

Hoplite greaves on display in Olympia, in southern Greece (left); a Corinthian helmet dating from about 500–490 B.C. (right).

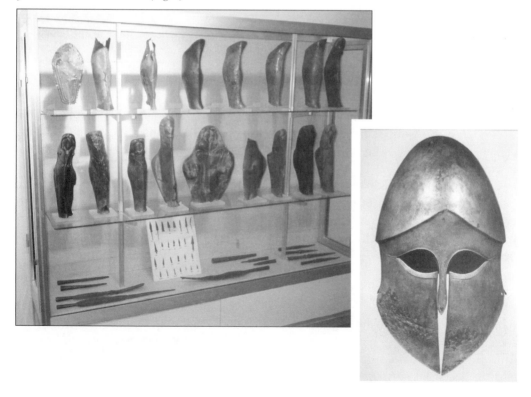

TRADITIONAL HOPLITE RITUALS

This excerpt from Thucydides's epic Pelo-ponnesian War (translated by Richard Craw-ley in The Landmark Thucydides*) vividly describes the Athenians' defeat by the Boeo-tians (Thebans) at the battle of Delium in the winter of 424 B.C. Mentioned are many standard rituals of hoplite warfare, including the paean, general's speech, running charge, othismos (shoving match), and erection of a victory trophy.*

On the side of the Athenians, the hoplites throughout the whole army formed eight [ranks] deep, being in numbers equal to the enemy. . . . The armies being now in line and upon the point of engaging, Hippocrates, the general, passed along the Athenian ranks, and encouraged them. . . . [He] had got half way through the army with his exhortation [pep talk], when the Boeotians . . . struck up the paean, and came against them from the hill; the Athenians advancing to meet them, and closing at a run. . . . [The armies] engaged with the utmost obstinacy [i.e., pushed against each other], shield against shield. The Boeotian left, as far as the center, was worsted by the Athenians. . . . Some of the Athenians also fell into confusion in surround-ing the enemy and mistook and so killed each other. . . . [On] the right, the Thebans . . . got the better of the Athenians and shoved them further and further back. . . . At length in both parts of the field . . . with their line broken by the advancing Thebans, the whole Athenian army took to flight. Some made for Delium and the sea . . . others for Mount Parnes, or wherever they had hopes of safety, pursued and cut down by the Boeotians. . . . The Boeotians set up a trophy, took up their own dead, and stripped those of the enemy.

or wrapped a bandanna around his head beneath the helmet.

A hoplite also wore bronze shin guards called greaves, which were often molded in the shape of leg muscles. In most cases he applied them by pulling them open and clipping them on, in the manner of mod-ern wrist and ear cuffs. A fabric lining helped reduce chafing, which must have been a persistent problem.

The hoplite's panoply was completed by his weapons, the principal one his thrusting-spear, which was about seven feet long. In addition to its iron head, it featured a sharp spike on the rear end. This provided a backup stabbing point in case the head broke off; the butt spike was also used to jab downward at enemies al-ready on the ground. The hoplite's iron sword, little changed from the slashing sword popular in the Dark Age, was about two feet long. He sheathed it in a scab-bard of wood covered by leather and used it primarily as a backup weapon when his spear was lost or broken.

Because this combination of arms and armor was so heavy and cumbersome, a hoplite usually donned it only shortly before battle. Whenever possible, he had a servant accompany him to carry the panoply and help him get into it. The re-lationship between warrior and servant was often close and interdependent. Ac-cording to the fifth-century B.C. Athenian historian Thucydides, for example, when Athenian hoplites were blockading an enemy town in 428 B.C., each received military pay of two drachmas a day, one for himself and one for his servant.[16] A servant also received one-half the food ration allotted to an Athenian hoplite.[17] When on the march, an army without servants was at a serious disadvantage, as illustrated by Thucydides' description of Athenian hoplites fleeing an army of Syracusans and Spartans in 413 B.C.:

> Dejection and self-condemnation were . . . rife among them. . . . The whole multitude on the march [was] not less than forty thousand men. All carried anything they could which might be of use, and the hoplites . . . contrary to their custom while under arms, carried their own provisions, in some cases for lack of servants, in others through not trusting them, as they [the servants] had long been deserting and now did so in greater numbers than ever.[18]

Organization of the Phalanx

The phalanx in which armored hoplites fought was essentially a long block of soldiers several ranks (lines) deep. A depth of eight ranks was most common. But on occasion there might be considerably more than eight or as few as three or four ranks. At Marathon (where the Athenians defeated an invading Persian army in 490 B.C.), for example, the Athenian commander thinned the center of his battle line to four or fewer ranks to make that line

match the mile-wide front of the larger Persian army. He did this to ensure that the enemy would not outflank, or move around and behind, his own army.

The ranks of hoplites within the phalanx were tightly organized into various divisions and units for maximum fighting efficiency. By the advent of the Classical Age, such organization varied somewhat from city to city. But scholars believe that all Greek phalanxes evolved from a basic prototype that developed during the late Dark Age and early Archaic Age. Presumably it was based on units of a hundred men, each unit called a *lochos*. This so-called archaic *lochos* probably broke down into various smaller units. Peter Connolly speculates that in battle the smallest units "would usually be drawn up in three files each of eight men, with the rear-rank officer standing clear at the back to make sure that the rear ranks did their job."[19]

Unfortunately, the exact organization of most of the Greek phalanxes of the Classical Age is uncertain. Sometimes this was the result of purposeful secrecy on the part of a city's military leaders. Sparta is a prime example. Its hoplites were widely feared and frequently successful on the battlefield, and its leaders wanted to keep their military edge over rival cities. The early Spartan phalanx may have consisted of five large units of a thousand men each. The fourth-century B.C. Athenian historian Xenophon, who resided in Sparta for a number of years, wrote that in his day Sparta's army was composed of large units about half that size.[20]

Scholars are much better informed about Athens's phalanx than those of other cities in the Classical Age. It consisted of

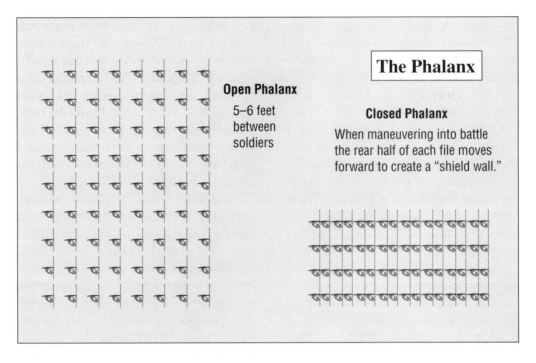

The Phalanx

Open Phalanx

5–6 feet between soldiers

Closed Phalanx

When maneuvering into battle the rear half of each file moves forward to create a "shield wall."

ten divisions, called *taxeis,* each commanded by a *taxiarchos.* Each *taxis* broke down into several *lochoi,* each perhaps consisting of a hundred men and supervised by a junior officer, the *lochagos.* The *taxiarchoi* and most other officers fought in the front rank, as did the *strategoi,* the generals to whom these officers reported. (Although Athens had ten *strategoi,* only three customarily accompanied the army on a campaign. One *strategos* was chosen as permanent commander in chief, or perhaps they rotated that position from day to day.) There were also a few rear-ranking *ouragoi* who supervised the rear of the phalanx.

Athenian military organization may have been fairly typical for a Greek city. However, the size of the Athenian phalanx was anything but typical; because Athens was by far the most populous city

in Greece, it could field larger armies, which often consisted of more than ten thousand hoplites. Even Sparta, which usually fielded only two to three thousand men at a time during the Classical Age, had a large army for a Greek city-state. Much more typical was Plataea, a city situated on the border between Attica and Boeotia; its entire army, which it sent to aid the Athenians at Marathon, consisted of between six hundred and a thousand hoplites.

The Phalanx in Action

The traditional Greek phalanx was an extremely effective offensive unit in its heyday (ca. 700–350 B.C.) for two reasons. First, it afforded its members a high degree of protection. When assembled in open order, they stood about five to six feet apart; but in close order—perhaps two to three feet apart, the mode most often adopted when closing with an enemy—their up-lifted shields created a formidable unbroken protective barrier. "Every shield protected not only its user's left side," Warry explains,

> but also the right side and lance arm of his neighbor. Once forma-tion was broken, this advantage was lost; the army which broke an enemy formation while preserving its own had won a battle. Once its own formation had been broken, an army usually took to flight.[21]

Defeated hoplites who did choose to make a run for it knew they could not get far bur-dened by their heavy panoply. The shield was usually the first item to be discarded. And the modern Greeks still use the term *ripsaspis,* "he who tosses away his shield," to denote a deserter. Widely famous was a ditty by the seventh-century B.C. poet Archilochus: "Well, what if some barbaric Thracian glories in the perfect shield I left under a bush? I was sorry to leave it—but I saved my skin. Does it matter? O hell, I'll buy a better one!"[22]

The other factor that made the phalanx so formidable was its tremendous and lethal forward momentum. As the forma-tion made contact with the enemy lines, the hoplites in the front rank jabbed their spears (overhanded) at their opponents, usually aiming for the belly, groin, or legs; at the same time, the hoplites in the rear

Greek hoplites drawn up in their characteristic phalanx (right) defeat the Persians at Plataea, in 479 B.C.

In this modern drawing, Greek warriors take prisoners following the Battle of Cunaxa, in Persia. Afterward, the Greek troops fought their way home through hundreds of miles of enemy territory.

ranks pushed at their comrades' backs, pressing them forward at the enemy. This maneuver was known as the *othismos,* "the shoving."

For all of these reasons, as the second-century B.C. Greek historian Polybius remarked, "So long as the phalanx retains its characteristic form and strength, nothing can withstand its charge or resist it face to face."[23] This was particularly true against non-Greeks. At Marathon, for instance, at the height of the battle, the Athenian wings, constituting small twin phalanxes, turned inward on the Persian center, and, like living steamrollers, crushed all in their path. At Cunaxa (in Persia) in 401

B.C., where Xenophon and other Greeks fought as mercenaries for a rebellious Persian prince, the opposing Persians were so frightened of the approaching phalanx that they simply ran away. Xenophon later recalled:

The two lines were hardly six or seven hundred yards apart when the Greeks began to chant the battle hymn and moved against the enemy. . . . Then altogether [they] broke into a ringing cheer, "Eleleu, eleleu!" and all charged at the double. . . . They also beat their spears on their shields to scare the horses. Before one shot reached them, the barbarians turned and fled. At once the Greeks pursued with might and main. . . . Not one Greek was hurt in this battle, except one on the left wing, said to have been shot by an arrow.[24]

The "battle hymn" (paean) and "cheer" (war cry) to which Xenophon refers were among various standard pre- , mid- , and postbattle practices undertaken by Greek hoplites. As they occurred in fairly rapid succession, these included sacrificing a goat or other animal just prior to battle to determine if the religious signs were favorable; listening to a spirit-raising speech by the commanding general; singing the paean to steel their nerves and intimidate the enemy; breaking into a running charge when coming within range of enemy archers; screaming the war cry during the

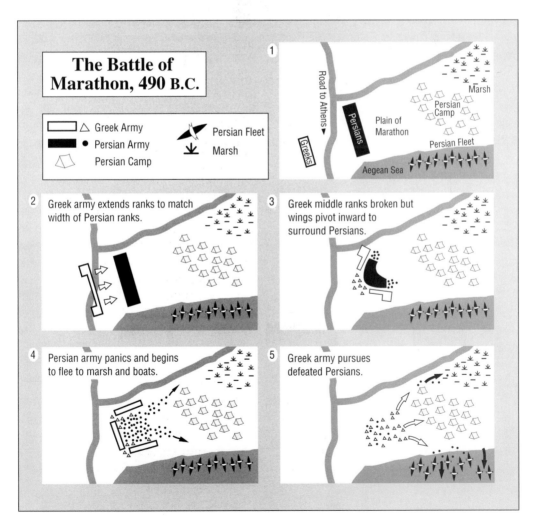

The Battle of Marathon, 490 B.C.

☐△ Greek Army
● Persian Army
🛆 Persian Camp
Persian Fleet
Marsh

1
Road to Athens ▼
Persians
Greeks
Plain of Marathon
Persian Camp
Marsh
Persian Fleet
Aegean Sea

2 Greek army extends ranks to match width of Persian ranks.

3 Greek middle ranks broken but wings pivot inward to surround Persians.

4 Persian army panics and begins to flee to marsh and boats.

5 Greek army pursues defeated Persians.

charge; engaging in the *othismos;* and if they were victorious, erecting on the battlefield a trophy (*tropaion*), a wooden framework displaying captured enemy arms, to give thanks to the gods.

The Dancing Floors of War

These practices, followed almost slavishly as a matter of tradition, illustrate the highly ritualistic nature of hoplite warfare. Indeed, after formal notification of battle, two Greek phalanxes faced each other on a predetermined, flat stretch of ground. (Several small plains bordering major city-states were used repeatedly; so many battles were fought on the great plain of Boeotia in the Classical Age that the Theban statesman Epaminondas called it the "dancing floor of war.") Like duelists settling a matter of honor, the formations then marched directly at each other, collided, and shoved each other back and forth until one side gave way.

In a very real way, this highly formal approach to fighting recalled the one-on-one duels between champions in Homer's *Iliad,* only with groups of men rather than single combatants. The analogy of the formal duel was certainly not lost on the classical Greeks. On at least one occasion in the early years of the phalanx, the opposing armies agreed to let a few chosen individuals decide the outcome of a contest. In 545 B.C., during a border dispute between Sparta and neighboring Argos, three hundred specially picked Spartans fought the same number of Argives. Both sides claimed victory in this so-called Battle of the Champions. (The argument led to a full-scale battle, which the Spartans won.)

 # THE BATTLE OF THE CHAMPIONS

Here, from his Histories, *the Greek historian Herodotus (often called the "father" of history) describes the unusual battle of Thyreatis, often called the Battle of the Champions, fought in the spring of 545 B.C.*

The Spartans were engaged in a quarrel with Argos over Thyreatis, a place in Argive territory [about halfway between the rival cities] which the Spartans had cut off and occupied. . . . The Argives marched to recover their stolen property, and agreed in conference with the Spartans that three hundred picked men from each side should fight it out and that Thyreatis should belong to the victors. So closely was the battle contested that of the six hundred men only three were left alive—two Argives . . . and one Spartan . . . and even these would have been killed had not darkness put an end to the fighting. The two Argives claimed the victory and hurried back to Argos; but the Spartan remained under arms and, having stripped the bodies of the Argive dead, carried their equipment to his own camp. Both parties met again on the following day. . . . For a while both [parties] maintained that they had won, the Argives because they had the greater number of survivors, the Spartans because their own man had remained on the battlefield. The argument ended in blows, and a fresh battle began, in which after severe losses on both sides, the Spartans were victorious.

As time went on, foreigners seeing or hearing about battles between phalanxes found them bizarre, to say the least. According to the fifth-century B.C. Greek historian Herodotus, a noted Persian general, Mardonius, told his king about the Greeks' "absurd notions of warfare," saying:

> When they declare war on each other, they go off together to the smoothest and most level piece of ground they can find, and have their battle on it. . . . Now surely, as they all talk the same language, they ought to be able to find a better way of settling their differences. . . . Or if it is really impossible to avoid coming to blows, they might at least employ the elements of strategy and look for a strong position to fight from.[25]

There was method in the madness of dueling phalanxes, however. The fighting was quick and decisive, usually resulted in minimal numbers of dead (thanks to the high degree of protection provided by the panoply), and almost always spared civilians and towns. So most of the time,

the agrarian farmer-fighters of Greece's Classical Age had the satisfaction of defending their territory and honor through combat, while managing to avoid prolonged, ruinous wars. "If hoplite fighting appeared absurd," Hanson points out, "at least it worked for a purpose—the preservation and expansion of an agrarian middle class."[26]

In any case, Mardonius's premature critique was based only on Greeks fighting other Greeks. He eventually learned the hard way how lethal Greek hoplites could be against non-Greeks when his army was nearly annihilated and he himself killed at Plataea in 479 B.C. In this great battle, the Greeks, fighting for their homes and way of life, fielded the largest army of hoplites in their history—probably more than sixty thousand in all. The victory forever ended Persian hopes of overrunning Europe; it also sent a message to other would-be conquerors, namely, that they would have to face the phalanx's frightening wall of bronze shields and raised spears. For more than two centuries following Plataea, says Hanson, "there was not an army in the world anywhere that was up to the task."[27]

CHAPTER THREE

Epaminondas to Alexander: A Revolution in Military Tactics

Traditional Greek hoplite warfare remained the premier fighting system in the Mediterranean sphere until the beginning of the fourth century B.C. But though highly effective, especially when used against non-Greeks, it still had considerable room for improvement. This is shown by a number of far-reaching changes and reforms in military units, tactics, and weapons that occurred in that pivotal century. A number of generals and other leaders from various Greek states played roles in this military revolution. But the major figures were Epaminondas, a Theban general and statesman; Philip II, king of Macedonia, a kingdom of northern Greece; and Philip's son, Alexander III, later called "the Great."

Rearranging the Phalanx

Epaminondas was instrumental in the introduction of the first of these military re-forms—a more effective strategy for deploying the phalanx. This development occurred as part of Thebes's response to Spartan tyranny. Sparta, whose phalanx was still the most feared in Greece, had defeated Athens in the horrific Peloponnesian War in 404 B.C. and assumed the hegemony (political and military dominance) of Greece. Thebes still held some modest local authority in Boeotia, where it had long been the recognized leader of the Boeotian League, a loose confederacy of about a dozen city-states.

Fearing the potential power of the Boeotian League, the Spartans arrogantly dissolved it in 386 B.C. And four years later, some fifteen hundred Spartan hoplites occupied the Theban acropolis in support of a Spartan-backed coup of Thebes's democratic government. Not surprisingly, existing local hatred of Sparta increased. So did patriotic resistance. In 379 B.C. Epaminondas's friend, the Theban leader Pelopidas, led a daring coup of his own, which overthrew the Spartan puppets and restored democracy. Soon afterward the Boeotian League was restored as well.

These events put Sparta and Thebes on a fateful collision course. In 371 B.C. one of Sparta's two kings (who ruled jointly), Cleombrotus, led a formidable force of hoplites toward Boeotia, bent on punishing Thebes. Preparing to meet this threat, the Thebans made Epaminondas the leading *boeotarch* (Theban general). Epaminondas and Pelopidas had been training the Theban troops for some time. Pelopidas had taken charge of the Sacred Band, a unit of three hundred elite fighters, each of whom was a match for the best Spartan hoplite.

Meanwhile, Epaminondas had drilled the main army in some new and unusual battlefield tactics. He had carefully observed the traditional way that Greek generals had arranged their infantry and noted that they placed their best troops on the right wing of the phalanx. When two opposing phalanxes met, the strong right wings always faced weaker enemy left wings; and the army with the most powerful right wing was usually able to crush the opposing left wing and then outflank the other army, assuring victory.

This nineteenth-century engraving depicts Epaminondas, the Theban military hero. Epaminondas's actual appearance is unknown.

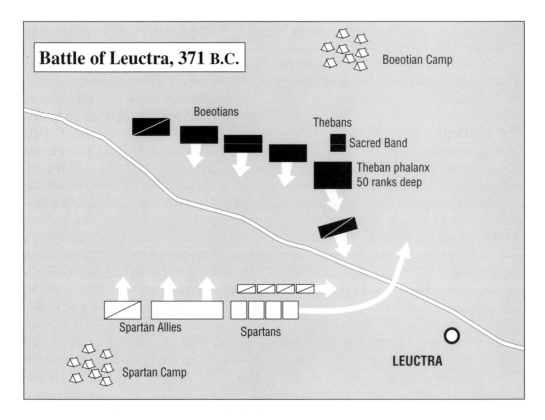

Battle of Leuctra, 371 B.C.

Boeotian Camp

Boeotians

Thebans

Sacred Band

Theban phalanx
50 ranks deep

Spartan Allies

Spartans

Spartan Camp

LEUCTRA

Epaminondas saw a way to change this tactical equation and its almost inevitable outcome. As Peter Connolly explains, he

believed that if he could knock out the crack Spartan troops on the right wing, the rest of the Spartan army would collapse. In order to achieve this, he planned to reverse his battle order, placing his own weakest troops on the right, opposite the Spartan left, lining up the phalanx *en echelon* [obliquely, or at an angle], with the weakest troops held back, whilst at the same time massing his best troops on the left, supported by the . . . Sacred Band.[28]

To give his left wing even more power, Epaminondas made it fifty rows deep, as compared to the twelve rows of the Spartan left wing. Fifty rows of hoplites shoving at their comrades' backs would obviously create more forward momentum than twelve.

The new Theban phalanx met its fateful test in July 371 B.C., near Leuctra, a village ten miles southwest of Thebes. Epaminondas's plan succeeded with brutal efficiency as the Theban left wing crushed the Spartan right. A thousand Spartans, including King Cleombrotus, were slain; while the Thebans lost only forty-seven men. In this single stroke, Epaminondas dispelled the myth of Spartan invincibility. Combined with a Theban follow-up expedition into Spartan territory a year later, the victory humbled Sparta (which never again rose to its former position of power and influence) and initiated a Theban hegemony of Greece.

The Macedonian Phalanx

Theban dominance was short-lived, however. Epaminondas died in battle in 362 B.C., and his countrymen lacked any leaders of his caliber to replace him. The next hegemony of Greece, which was fated to last much longer, was that of Macedonia. During one of Thebes's many police actions during its brief but vigorous period of supremacy, Macedonia's Prince Philip, then a teenager, was taken to Thebes as a hostage. During his three-year stay in that city, the boy received the respect and kind treatment befitting his rank as an aristocrat. He stayed in the home of Pammenes, a *boeotarch* and close associate of Epaminondas. Exactly how much military science Philip learned directly from Pammenes and Epaminondas is unclear. But there is no doubt that Philip's later military tactics reflected Epaminondas's influence, even if indirectly.[29]

Whatever his inspiration, Philip proved to be a gifted military tactician and innovator, unquestionably the greatest Europe had produced up to that time. When he ascended the throne in 359 B.C. (after returning to Macedonia following his release by the Thebans), Macedonia was a disunited, culturally backward kingdom on the fringe of the Greek world and had a small, largely ineffective army. With amazing speed, he unified the country's feuding regions and tribes into a single, powerful nation. His principal tool in this endeavor was a truly professional army, Europe's first. In sharp contrast to the militias utilized by the city-states, which were called up only when needed, his soldiers made up a permanent, standing force and received extensive training.

THE SHOWDOWN AT LEUCTRA

The first-century B.C. Greek historian Diodorus Siculus left behind this description (from volume 7 of his Library of History*) of the battle in which Epaminondas ended the Spartan hegemony over Greece.*

When the trumpets on both sides sounded the charge and the armies simultaneously with the first onset raised the battle cry . . . they met in hand-to-hand combat, [and] at first both fought ardently and the battle was evenly poised; shortly, however, as Epaminondas's men began to derive advantage from . . . the denseness of their lines [i.e., the depth of the phalanx], many Peloponnesians [the Spartans and their allies] began to fall. For they were unable to endure the weight of the courageous fighting of the elite corps [the Sacred Band]. . . . The Spartans were with great difficulty forced back; at first, as they gave ground they would not break their formation, but finally, as many fell and the commander who would have rallied them [Cleombrotus] had died, the army turned and fled in utter rout.

Philip also introduced a much-improved military system that in time became highly integrated; that is, instead of relying mainly on the phalanx, it consisted of several different elements, each of which supported and strengthened the others. First, Philip made the traditional phalanx more formidable. He deepened its ranks to a standard sixteen. And he greatly increased the length of the soldiers' spears, from about eight to nearly eighteen feet. These two-handed pikes, called *sarissas,* weighed about fifteen pounds and required two hands to hold and maneuver properly. The ends of the pikes held by the men in the first five rows projected horizontally from

the front of the phalanx, forming an impenetrable, hedgehog-like mass of sharpened metal. Meanwhile, the soldiers in the back rows held their *sarissas* at more upward angles, creating a forest of points that helped deflect incoming arrows and other missiles.

Philip made other changes in the standard phalanx. The men in the first few rows retained a fair amount of armor; but those in the rear eleven rows, who rarely made contact with the enemy, wore little or no armor. And to give his pikemen a sense of prestige, and thereby increase morale, Philip called them the king's "foot-companions" (*pezetairoi*). To

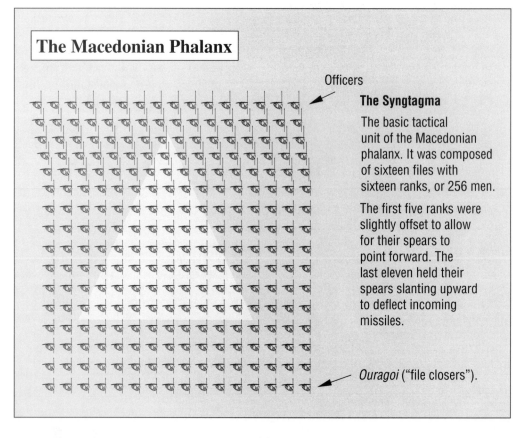

The Macedonian Phalanx

Officers

The Syntagma

The basic tactical unit of the Macedonian phalanx. It was composed of sixteen files with sixteen ranks, or 256 men.

The first five ranks were slightly offset to allow for their spears to point forward. The last eleven held their spears slanting upward to deflect incoming missiles.

Ouragoi ("file closers").

One of Philip's companion cavalrymen manages to hold his spear and rein in his horse at the same time. These armored horsemen were trained to charge at enemy infantry formations.

outsiders, the new formation became known, appropriately, as the Macedonian phalanx.

New Cavalry Units

Another key element in Philip's new integrated arms system was an elite cavalry corps of young noblemen (which his ancestor, Alexander I, had introduced). Known as the companion cavalry (*hetairoi*), this force

had long been used mainly to guard the king and had played little role in actual battle. Indeed, Greek cavalry (*hippeis*) had come into common use only in the late fifth century B.C. And even then, it was not employed in large-scale shock action (direct charges on infantry). First, horses were not plentiful in most parts of southern Greece; also, saddles and stirrups had not yet been invented, so that riders had difficulty staying on swiftly

UNARMED ROCK THROWERS

Military historians usually devote much space to the phalanx, cavalry, and peltasts, and rightly so. But often forgotten are the ordinary citizens who could not afford armor and weapons but often followed and supported armies on the march. In this excerpt from his informative Warriors of Ancient Greece, *historian Nicholas Sekunda describes these rock-throwing* psiloi.

Greek *psiloi* are normally shown [in ancient vase paintings] wearing the everyday dress of Greek shepherds: a tunic of coarse cloth and a shaggy felt hat. . . . One feature nearly all have in common is that they carry a makeshift shield formed by an animal pelt laid along the left arm and secured in place by knotting a pair of paws

around the neck. . . . Occasions did occur when even the humble rock could be used to effect against a hoplite army. In 457 B.C., the Corinthians . . . descended on Megara [a city northwest of Athens], thinking that the Athenians were too heavily committed to campaigns elsewhere. But the Athenians called out the young men between 18 and 20 and the old men between 50 and 60. . . . The Corinthian hoplites were thrown back, and in their confusion a considerable proportion of them lost their way and rushed into some farmland enclosed by a great ditch. It was a dead end. The Athenians shut them in with hoplites; then the *psiloi* who had followed the expedition stoned to death the Corinthian hoplites trapped inside.

moving horses. So the Greeks had used cavalry mainly to protect the phalanx against enemy skirmishers (javelin throwers and archers), to chase down escaping enemy hoplites after the phalanxes had fought, and to rescue their own injured or escaping hoplites. Xenophon had advocated that a horseman carry two javelins. "For the skillful man," he wrote,

> may throw the one and can use the other in front or on either side or behind. They are also stronger than the spear and easier to manage. We recommend [the horseman] throwing the javelin at the longest range possible. For this gives a man more time to turn his horse and to grasp the other javelin.[30]

Such weapons and tactics would obviously have had little or no effect on the solid bronze wall of the phalanx.

Under Philip, however, horsemen began to come into their own. He placed his *hetairoi* on the largest mounts available and dressed the riders in armor, including bronze helmets, breastplates, and greaves. And he trained them to charge in a wedge-shaped formation directly at enemy infantry. Though these horsemen could not defeat a phalanx all by themselves, they *could* punch a hole in the armored line; the Macedonian phalanx could then exploit that breach, splitting the enemy army down the middle. As part of the integrated system, therefore, the cavalry "softened up" the enemy for the attack of the phalanx that followed.

Peltasts and Other Light-Armed Troops

Philip supported his "one-two" punch of cavalry and infantry with offensive units of light-armed soldiers that are often referred to collectively as skirmishers. Besides archers, these included slingers (who used leather slings to hurl small rocks or lumps of lead up to a thousand feet or more); *psiloi* (men who hurled rocks with their bare hands); and peltasts (*peltastai*). Peltasts were named for their characteristic small round or crescent-shaped wicker shield, the *pelta* (which hung by a strap on the back when not in use). Wearing no armor, they carried small bundles of javelins, and their chief tactic was to approach the enemy, throw their weapons, and then run away.

An unarmored fighter, one of the skirmishers known as psiloi, *prepares to hurl a rock.*

As in the case of horsemen, the Greeks made little use of such light-armed troops until the late fifth century B.C. Their weapons posed little threat to the phalanx, and generals usually employed them to guard the wings of that formation against horsemen and other skirmishers. Most skirmishers were mercenaries. The archers came mostly from Crete, the slingers from Rhodes (off the southwestern coast of Asia Minor), and the peltasts from Thrace (on the Aegean's northern rim). In 390 B.C. an Athenian general named Iphicrates used a specially trained group of Thracian peltasts to defeat a small force of Spartan hoplites. After that, Athens and other Greek states increased their use of these skirmishers. (Athens eventually began recruiting peltasts from its poorer classes to supplement the mercenaries it continued to import.) In an attempt to counter their effect, generals chose a few of their youngest and fastest hoplites. These men became known as *ekdromoi,* or "runners out," because they left the formation and chased after the peltasts. Normal hoplite armor would have unduly slowed down an *ekdromos,* so he wore a much reduced and lighter panoply.

HOPLITES DEFEATED BY PELTASTS

From his Hellenica *(Rex Warner's translation), Xenophon here describes the defeat of a group of some six hundred Spartan hoplites by peltasts commanded by the Athenian general Iphicrates outside the walls of the Greek city of Corinth in 390 B.C.*

Iphicrates . . . saw that the Spartans were neither in great force nor protected by peltasts or cavalry, and came to the conclusion that it would be safe to attack them with [his] own peltasts. If they marched along the road, they could be shot at with javelins on their unprotected side and mowed down; and if they tried to pursue their attackers, it would be perfectly easy for the peltasts, light and fast on their feet, to keep out of the way of the hoplites. . . . Iphicrates with his peltasts attacked the regiment of Spartans. And now as the javelins were hurled at them, some of the Spartans were killed and some wounded. . . . The polemarch [Spartan commander] then ordered the infantry in the age groups 20 to 30 to charge and drive off their attackers. However, they were hoplites pursuing peltasts at a distance of a javelin's throw, and they failed to catch anyone. . . . When the Spartans . . . turned back from the pursuit, Iphicrates' men wheeled round, some hurling their javelins again from in front while others ran up along the flank, shooting at the side [of the Spartan formation] unprotected by the shields. . . . Then, as things were going very badly, the polemarch ordered another pursuit. . . . But in falling back from this pursuit even more men were killed than before. . . . The Spartans were already at their wits' end . . . and now when, in addition to all this, they saw hoplites [from the city] bearing down on them, they broke and ran. . . . In all the fighting and in the flight about two hundred and fifty of them were killed.

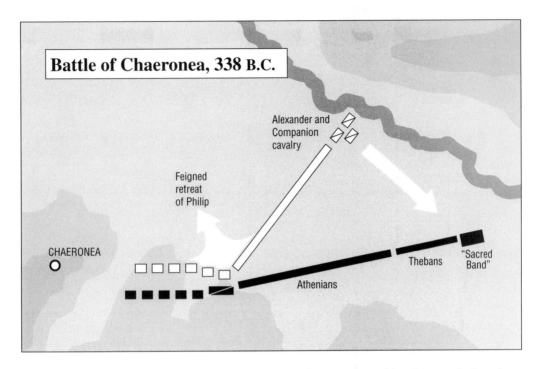

Battle of Chaeronea, 338 B.C.

Alexander and Companion cavalry

Feigned retreat of Philip

CHAERONEA

Thebans

"Sacred Band"

Athenians

Philip recruited and trained large numbers of peltasts and other skirmishers. Like earlier Greek generals, he used them to guard the flanks of his infantry. But he also had them provide an initial bombardment to hold the enemy line at bay and prepare the way for the frontal assault of his companion cavalry.

A New Goal for Greek Armies

As if these military reforms were not enough, Philip introduced into Western warfare a new philosophy and goal of battle—conquest—as opposed to turf battles among farming communities. Under his influence, warfare "became much more than personal courage, nerve, and physical strength," Victor Hanson points out.

Nor was killing by Macedonians just over territorial borders. Rather,

the strategy of battle was designed predominantly as an instrument of ambitious state policy. . . . Philip's territorial ambitions had nothing to do with a few acres outside the city-state, but rather encompassed a broader vision of mines, harbors, and tribute-paying communities that might be his solely to fuel his rapacious [victory-hungry] army.[31]

Indeed, Philip used his new integrated military system (along with some shrewd diplomacy and out-and-out trickery) to seize hegemony over the once powerful city-states of southern Greece. In the summer of 338 B.C., a hastily formed alliance of these cities, led by Athens and Thebes, attempted to stop him at Chaeronea, in western Boeotia. Placing a mass of skirmishers and light-armed hoplites on his

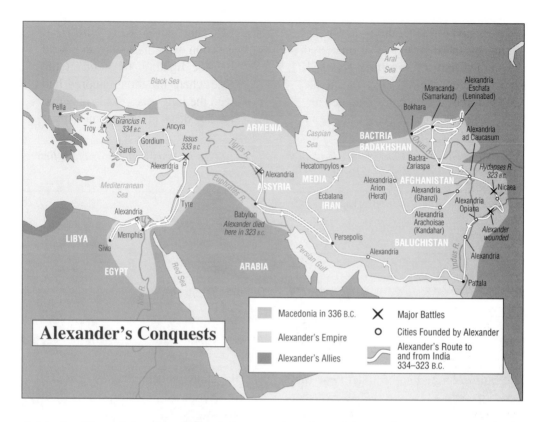

Alexander's Conquests

right wing beyond the edge of his phalanx, Philip slanted the rest of the phalanx back at an oblique angle, as Epaminondas had at Leuctra. Leading the right wing himself, the king pretended to retreat. This lured the Athenians into a wild charge, separating them from the Thebans and other allies and opening a gap in the allied line. The Macedonian companion cavalry, which had been stationed on the left wing, then charged into the gap, led by the eighteen-year-old Prince Alexander. Meanwhile, Philip and his phalanx suddenly halted the feigned retreat and went on the attack, impaling many of the oncoming Athenians on massed pikes. As the Athenians and other allies broke and ran, the Macedonians surrounded the The-

ban Sacred Band, the only allied unit that stood its ground. These truly brave men fought to the death; but their sacrifice was in vain, for Philip's victory over the city-states was complete and decisive.

In a way, the heroic last stand of the Sacred Band symbolized the last gasp of the old Greek ideal of citizen-hoplites assembling mainly to defend their local turf. Philip, whose new military ethic of broader conquest would replace it and become a model for future Western imperialists, was astounded at the Thebans' bravery. According to the first-century A.D. Greek biographer Plutarch:

The Sacred Band . . . consisted of three hundred picked men, who were given their training and lodging by the city and were quartered on the Cadmea [the central fortress]. . . . According to some accounts, this force . . . was never defeated until the battle of Chaeronea. The story goes that when King Philip of Macedon was inspecting the dead after the fighting, he stood at the place where the three hundred had faced the long pikes of his phalanx, and lay dead in their armor, their

Alexander and troops charge up the bank of the Granicus River, in Asia Minor, scene of his first great victory in his conquest of Persia.

bodies piled one upon the other. He was amazed at the sight.[32]

Philip's Army Passes to Alexander

In the wake of Chaeronea, the city-states found themselves swept along in the tide of Philip's grandiose plans for invading Persia. As it turned out, however, Philip did not end up leading this fateful expedition. In 336 B.C. a disgruntled Macedonian stabbed him to death, and Alexander found himself both king of Macedonia and captain-general of the new Greek confederacy Philip had forged.

Two years later, Alexander initiated the great military campaigns that subsequently brought all the lands stretching from Greece to India under his authority. Much has been made over the years of his genius as a military commander. His overall strategies and deployment of his highly integrated forces on the battlefield were certainly adept, if not at times brilliant. But how much of this can be attributed to him personally and how much to his father's influence and that of Philip's seasoned generals, who accompanied the young king into Persia? As noted military historian J.F.C. Fuller suggests, "Alexander's greatest asset was the army he inherited from his father; without it, in spite of his genius, his conquests would be inconceivable—it was an instrument exactly suited to his craft."[33] Hanson agrees, calling Alexander "an energetic, savvy adolescent, who inherited from his father a frighteningly murderous army and the loyal cadre [group] of very shrewd and experienced battle administrators who

knew how to take such a lethal show on the road."[34]

Because firm evidence for the exact sources of Alexander's military ideas is lacking, the question of who was the more gifted general—he or his father—must remain a matter of academic debate. What is certain is that in his Asian campaigns, Alexander employed Philip's army and battlefield tactics often and with distinction, at times improving on those tactics. Typically, the young commander used his companion cavalry for shock action against Persian infantry, as his father had taught him. One of Alexander's innovations was to place his best cavalry unit on his right wing, along with his light infantry and skirmishers, and to lead the initial attack with these horsemen; meanwhile, he usually angled the rest of his forces backward toward the left as Epaminondas and Philip had done.

Also essential to Alexander's success was a phenomenally well-coordinated system of supply depots, which his operatives forced local officials to set up in advance of the army. Without them, he could not have sustained that army, which used in excess of 250 tons of grain and seventy thousand gallons of water per day.

Perhaps Alexander's main and most lasting achievement was to spread the new Macedonian military system (as well as Greek political and cultural ideas) beyond Greece's borders and across the Near East. He clearly demonstrated the superiority of Greek armies over non-Greek ones. And had he lived longer, he may well have used that superiority to bring all of Europe under his control. (Evidence shows that he planned to march westward into Europe after consolidating his eastern empire.) However, Alexander died unexpectedly at the age of thirty-three in June 323 B.C. The Macedonian military system then became a horribly destructive tool in the hands of his generals, most of whom proved to be every bit as ruthless as he. An age in which the art of killing would be raised to new heights was about to begin.

CHAPTER FOUR

Mercenaries and Siege Machines: War in the Hellenistic Age

Alexander's ideas and tactics (and indirectly Philip's) provided a bridge, both political and military, between the classical era of city-states and what modern scholars call the Hellenistic Age (323–30 B.C.). Though he died young, Alexander's shadow hovered over and in large degree shaped the rulers and policies of the new age. Macedonian military might had overcome the city-states; most of these had been small, run by democratic citizen-bodies and institutions, and uninterested in large-scale conquest. By contrast, Alexander was a king; he ruled by a combination of divine right and autocratic means, and his policies were based on extending his authority over others and amassing an empire. His leading generals and governors, who became known as the Successors, adopted his system. And the Hellenistic Age saw the eastern Mediterranean and Near East dominated by a series of large Greek kingdoms.

To advance their imperial goals, carve out and maintain their realms, and settle their rivalries, the Hellenistic monarchs waged a long series of brutal wars against one another. Such efforts naturally required effective, murderous weapons and armies. On the one hand, these rulers had inherited from Philip and Alexander the most sophisticated and lethal military system in the world. On the other, the Successors expanded on that system, spending enormous amounts of money to create ever-larger, more destructive weapons and armies.

Indeed, size became the hallmark of Hellenistic warfare. Armies continued to utilize the phalanx of pikemen, shock cavalry units, and other features of the integrated Macedonian system; but what made these armies different was that they were often huge by former standards. At the battle of Ipsus, fought in 301 B.C. between two of the Successors—Antigonus and Seleucus—the two forces totaled almost a quarter of a million men. Not surprisingly, the number of dead in such battles was also larger—often in the tens of thousands for a single engagement. In addition, massive sieges were undertaken, for which giant siege machines were constructed; while fortifications underwent a corresponding increase in size and sophistication to meet this challenge. Warships increased in size and number as well. And generals began to press into battlefield service the largest living land animal—the elephant.

An Increased Use of Mercenaries

Another important hallmark of Hellenistic warfare was the mercenary soldier. The city-states had used mercenaries in the Classical Age, but mainly in supplementary or supporting units. (The most common examples had been archers from Crete, slingers from Rhodes, and peltasts from Thrace.) The Hellenistic states, by contrast, manned their armies, including their phalanxes, *primarily* with mercenaries.

The main reason for this transition to reliance on mercenary soldiers was money. First, the Greek kingdoms were rich, partly from the vast amounts of gold and other valuables captured from Persian treasuries,

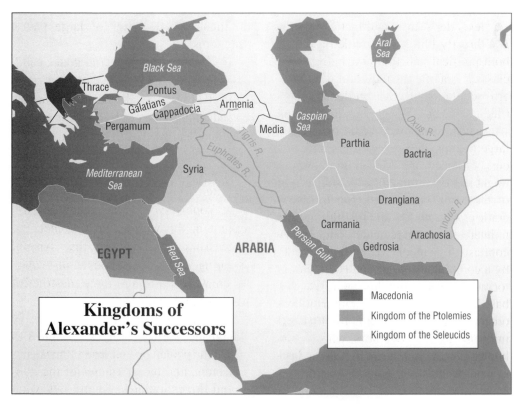

Kingdoms of Alexander's Successors

Macedonia
Kingdom of the Ptolemies
Kingdom of the Seleucids

Following the Battle of Cunaxa, in 401 B.C., Xenophon and his mercenary army rejoice on reaching the Black Sea following their dangerous overland trek.

and also from new property and income taxes the autocratic kings forced on their subjects. Second, the prospect of booty—valuables and goods plundered from the enemy—lured young men from far and wide. Many came from former Persian lands, or from as far away as India and Africa. But many others were former Greek farmers. The chance to get rich or at least earn a regular living fighting for some warlord now seemed preferable to breaking one's back on the land and forfeiting a large portion of the profits to heavy taxation.

The use of mercenaries was only one of the ways that the money flowing from and through the Hellenistic kingdoms reflected "the extraordinary degree to which Greek culture had become militarized," in Victor Hanson's words. "The continual enslavement of captured peoples," he adds,

> and the subsequent greater use of slaves in both agriculture and manufacturing . . . meant a growing urbanism [trend toward larger cities]. . . .

Thus, there was a rich pool of itinerant craftsmen, mercenaries, and skilled workers who were less concerned with civic government and [supporting citizen assemblies and juries]. Instead, royal regimes attracted talent for military construction and service and left the bothersome business of politics to their own courts. Available capital for war then increased. . . . Less money was needed for the participation of fewer citizens in municipal government . . . and more was gained by allowing innovative and ruthless men to mount invasions that were little more than organized robberies.[35]

One major problem with this new money-driven war mentality was trying to maintain the allegiance of and control over one's own hired thugs. When farmer-hoplites had gone to war to defend their own homes and lands, loyalty to the state and to one's comrades on the field had been taken more or less for granted. In contrast, mercenary troops could only be counted on if the potential profits were great enough; also, the lure of said profits made these soldiers difficult to manage and unreliable, even in the midst of battle. "This fact goes far to explaining why the wars which they fought were usually so inconclusive," John Warry points out.

A mercenary force possessed of the baggage train of a defeated army—let alone a town or territory which had sheltered the enemy—in its

A TREMENDOUS BARRAGE

One of the most famous, and certainly one of the most spectacular, of the sieges of Hellenistic times took place in 213–212 B.C., when the brilliant Greek inventor Archimedes utilized ingenious devices and techniques to defend his native Syracuse against a force of attacking Romans. In his biography of the Roman commander Marcellus (translated by Ian Scott-Kilvert in Makers of Rome*), Plutarch wrote:*

Archimedes brought his engines to bear and launched a tremendous barrage against the Roman army. This consisted of a variety of missiles, including a great volley of stones [thrown by catapults larger and more lethal than any yet invented] which descended upon their target with an incredible noise and velocity. There was no protection against this artillery, and the soldiers were knocked down in swathes and their ranks thrown into confusion. At the same time huge beams were run out from the walls so as to project over the Roman ships: some of them were then sunk by great weights dropped from above, while others were seized at the bows by iron claws . . . hauled into the air . . . until they stood upright upon their sterns, and then allowed to plunge . . . [until they were] dashed against the steep cliffs and rocks.

preoccupation with plunder would have little incentive to follow up a victory or pursue fugitives. Indeed, it was hardly in the mercenary's interest to eliminate the opposing forces completely. By doing so, he would have deprived himself of employment and so a living.[36]

An Array of Lethal Siege Devices

The large sums of money spent by the Hellenistic realms on conquest and defense was also reflected in an increased emphasis on siege warfare, which they elevated to a high art. Greek inventors, engineers, and machinists produced a wide

array of lethal devices. These included enormous siege towers that moved on giant wheels, huge drills that could pierce stone walls, and sophisticated catapults and other mechanical missile throwers (artillery).

Sieges had been an occasional feature of Greek warfare ever since the Bronze Age. But those involving siege towers, artillery, and other large-scale devices became common only after the mid–fourth century B.C., when Philip showed their effectiveness in his sieges of the cities of Olynthus (349 B.C.) and Perinthus (340 B.C.). Alexander's subsequent successful sieges of Halicarnassus (334 B.C.) and Tyre (332 B.C.) became the models followed by the Hellenistic generals.

These Greek siege devices hurled stones and arrow-like darts by means of springs fashioned of bundles of twisted sinew or hair.

HELLENISTIC FORTIFICATIONS

In the two centuries following Philip and Alexander, the design of Greek fortresses and their walls underwent a transformation in response to innovations in offensive siege engines and techniques. Here, from his Greece and Rome at War, *Peter Connolly describes some of these improvements in fortifications.*

There was only one real answer to the new siege techniques and this was to keep the enemy away from the walls. . . . Catapults could be used for defense as well as offense, and from the middle of the fourth century B.C. walls and towers were designed to hold artillery. Both were pierced with loopholes and artillery ports. The towers were often as many as four or five stories high, with heavy artillery at second-floor level and lighter pieces at the top. . . . A pitched roof [was constructed] at the top of the towers, primarily to protect the defenders from the [attackers'] stone-throwers. . . . A large ditch (or series of ditches) was dug in front of the walls . . . to make it more difficult to bring up siege engines. . . . Beyond the trenches were covered holes and artificial marshes to trap the machines. The city walls were thickened and heightened . . . [and] the gates were massively reinforced. The north gate at Selinus, in Sicily, has a complex system of outworks [battlements projecting outward from the walls] forcing a would-be attacker to run the gauntlet before reaching the gates. The entrance to these outworks was defended by an artillery battery.

All of these individuals owed much to an earlier Greek military genius— Dionysius I. In 405 B.C. he became dictator and military commander of the powerful Sicilian Greek city of Syracuse. Dionysius offered hefty rewards to inventors to come up with new siege devices, and by 397 B.C. he was able to mount a devastating attack on the Carthaginian city of Motya. In the Syracusan arsenal were siege towers six stories high that moved on wheels and hundreds of mechanical crossbows. The bows themselves were large versions of the standard composite bow used for centuries; each was attached to a wooden framework equipped with a metal winch that slowly drew back the bowstring. A barrage of wooden bolts shot by these bows showered the city's battlements; that reduced the number of traditional arrows and rocks fired by the defenders, allowing the siege towers to get close to the walls. The well-fortified towers provided cover for men operating large battering rams. Once these rams smashed their way in, Dionysius ordered the towers into the town and these dropped wooden gangways onto the rooftops; his troops then poured out of the towers and took control of the buildings.

These devices and tactics remained basic to Philip, Alexander, and the Successors, although their sieges did utilize other elements. Common was mining (digging tunnels), aimed either at weakening and collapsing a city's defensive walls or transporting troops beneath them. The defenders often tried to counter the mines by filling them with smoke, digging deep moats around their walls (so that the mines could not reach them), or undermining the tunnels with mines of their own. Greek inventors also introduced torsion-powered catapults. These devices featured bundles of animal tendons or human hair that had been twisted tightly; once released, the pent-up energy propelled large bolts or stones a half a mile or more. Needless to say,

the impact of such missiles often did serious damage to stone walls.

The Siege of Rhodes

All of these devices and methods were exploited in the largest and most famous siege of the age—that of the main fortress of Rhodes by Demetrius, son of one of Alexander's most important generals, Antigonus. Rhodes was one of the few city-states that remained a viable power alongside the great kingdoms in early Hellenistic times. This was mainly due to the island's powerful navy, the best in the east-

In this modern engraving Demetrius's ships, equipped with siege towers, approach the Rhodian fortifications. Through skill, bravery, and sheer tenacity, the Rhodians kept the enemy at bay.

60

ern Mediterranean. At first, the Rhodians refused to ally themselves with any of the Successors and thereby managed to steer clear of their destructive conflicts. Finally, though, they sided with Ptolemy, who had established himself as ruler of Egypt.

In response, Ptolemy's principal military opponents, Antigonus and Demetrius, decided to punish Rhodes. In 305 B.C. Demetrius assembled a vast invasion force, consisting of more than 350 of his own ships, hundreds of pirate ships, and more than a thousand private craft. Like his mercenaries, the pirates and private citizens who followed him hoped to cash in on the spoils when he sacked the main city and sold its inhabitants into slavery.

The plan of the siege was twofold. Demetrius landed an army, which plundered villages and farmland before setting up a camp some distance from the city's defensive walls. Meanwhile, more of his men constructed a small harbor for his ships (since the Rhodians had fortified and blocked off their own main harbor to keep the invaders out). Some of Demetrius's troops managed to secure a beachhead on the mole (artificial pier of piled stones and earth) at the front of the main harbor; but the defenders rushed their own troops to the spot and kept the attackers in check. Similarly, when Demetrius's miners tried to tunnel under the walls, the Rhodians stopped them by excavating their own mines. Demetrius ordered in catapults and other artillery. But the Rhodians had artillery pieces of their own, which they mounted on platforms on the decks of ships; these devices showered large darts and rocks

onto Demetrius's ships when they tried to penetrate the main harbor.

The "City-Taker"

The Rhodian defenders seemed able to counter every offensive move Demetrius made. So he brought up his secret weapon, the most sensational siege weapon in the annals of ancient warfare. He and his engineers called it the Helepolis, or "City-taker." It was, as Plutarch recorded, an immense

> siege tower with a square base, each side of which measured seventy-two feet at the bottom. It was ninety-nine feet high with the upper part tapering off to narrower dimensions. Inside, it was divided into many separate stories and compartments, the side which faced the enemy being pierced with apertures on each story through which missiles could be discharged, and it was manned with troops who were equipped with every kind of weapon. The machine never tottered or leaned in any direction, but rolled forwards firm and upright on its base, advancing with an even motion and with a noise and an impetus that inspired mingled feelings of alarm and delight in all who beheld it.[37]

Plutarch says the tower had "many separate stories." Other ancient writers, including the first-century B.C. Greek Diodorus Siculus, are a bit more specific. From them we learn that the Helepolis had nine stories; they also record its height at between 130 and 140 feet. Plutarch's lower estimate of ninety-nine feet may be a mistake based on figures

A modern artist's conception of Demetrius's "City-taker." According to ancient writers, it took more than three thousand men to move the huge device.

for a smaller (but still impressive) siege tower that Demetrius built for an earlier siege. Diodorus also asserts that it took some thirty-four hundred men to move the Helepolis. Further, its front and sides were covered with iron plates to protect it from flaming arrows, which might have ignited and burned its timber framework. The front featured numerous ports, each covered with

a shutter made of animal hides to keep out arrows and other missiles. Through these ports, Demetrius's soldiers fired catapults and other artillery.

According to Diodorus's account, the mammoth City-taker slowly approached the city's defensive perimeter. Eight penthouses accompanied the tower, four on each side. These were wooden galleries, also on wheels and covered on the top and sides by animal hides reinforced with bundles of seaweed or straw. The penthouses protected the soldiers entering, exiting, and pushing the siege tower. Two larger covered structures, each containing a huge battering ram with a metal tip, also moved alongside the Helepolis.

When this formidable array of engines came in range of the walls, the artillery inside the tower unleashed a deadly rain of bolts and rocks onto the battlements. This sent the defenders scurrying and soon destroyed an entire section of wall. Meanwhile, however, the Rhodians had already begun countering the threat by erecting a second wall inside the first. That night the defenders also sent out a force of commandos that attacked the tower; and though they

This modern reconstruction of the famous Colossus of Rhodes incorrectly depicts it as gigantic and straddling the harbor entrance. The real statue was smaller and stood with its legs together.

failed to set it afire, they apparently did enough damage to force Demetrius to order it back out of range. When it was repaired, though, he ordered it forward again. Once more, it did severe damage to some sections of wall. But when Demetrius sent a squad of troops into the breach, the Rhodians, in an incredible display of desperate and heroic fighting, repelled them with heavy losses.

In the end the defenders' stubbornness, ingenuity, and courage prevailed. After several months Demetrius finally realized that he could not take the city and left. Still, the sheer size and audacity of his effort earned him the nickname of Poliorcetes, "the Besieger," by which posterity came to know him.

As for the triumphant Rhodians, they celebrated their deliverance in a manner as spectacular as the attack itself. They gathered up the enormous amount of bronze from the siege engines the enemy had left behind and melted it down. Then, befitting the Hellenistic emphasis on largeness, they erected a giant statue at the edge of their harbor. A 110-foot-high image of the sun god, Helios (their patron deity), it became known as the Colossus of Rhodes and one of the Seven Wonders of the Ancient World.

Battle Elephants

Still another example of the Hellenistic generals' obsession with weapons of great size—battle elephants—made a short but big splash in European warfare during the age of the Successors and their offspring. The Greeks did not invent this rather unorthodox mode of warfare. Rather, they first encountered battle elephants when

Alexander squared off against the Persians at Gaugamela (in Mesopotamia) in 331 B.C. The Persians themselves had gotten the idea from neighboring India. And when Alexander eventually marched into India, the enemy employed more than two hundred elephants against his army at the Hydapses River. According to Alexander's Greek biographer Arrian:

> The elephant-drivers forced their beasts to meet the opposing cavalry, while the Macedonian infantry, in its turn, advanced against them, shooting down the drivers, and pouring a hail of missiles from every side upon the elephants themselves. It was an odd bit of work—quite unlike any previous battle; the monster elephants plunged this way and that among the lines of infantry, dealing destruction . . . and as they blundered about . . . they trampled to death as many of their friends as their enemies. The result was that the Indian cavalry, jammed in around the elephants and with no more space than they had, suffered severely. . . . Riderless and bewildered . . . and maddened by pain and fear, [the beasts ran amok], thrusting, trampling, and spreading death before them.[38]

Arrian's description is valuable in that it reveals some of the strengths of using elephants in battle as well as some of the weaknesses. The huge creatures could trample foot soldiers; they could also be trained to pick up men with their trunks

An armored battle elephant tramples an enemy cavalryman in this modern depiction of a Hellenistic battle. These beasts sometimes panicked and killed soldiers from their own army.

and toss them to the ground. In addition, elephants often frightened the horses of enemy cavalry units, sending those units into flight. When Alexander's cousin Pyrrhus of Epirus sent in elephants against an army of Romans unfamiliar with the beasts, the results were decisive. The Roman horses panicked, and Pyrrhus took advantage of their disarray by launching an attack of his own cavalry against them, winning the battle. One of the most renowned of the Hellenistic generals, Pyrrhus was also credited with introducing the idea of mounting armored towers on the backs of battle elephants. This, Warry points out,

offered a higher platform from which missiles could be launched. The turret . . . might accommodate a crew of four. . . . The ancients attached great importance to a point of vantage based on superior height. The archer who threatened his enemy from above gained a wider view and a greater range.[39]

As Arrian's account reminds us, though, battle elephants had just as many disadvantages as advantages. They could be wounded and killed by massed attack by archers, peltasts, and other skirmishers; and the pikes of the Macedonian

PYRRHUS'S ELEPHANTS
SECURE A VICTORY

In this excerpt from his biography of the Hellenistic military general Pyrrhus (translated by Ian Scott-Kilvert in The Age of Alexander), *Plutarch tells how the Greek elephants caused disorder in the Roman ranks at the battle of Heraclea (in southern Italy) in 280 B.C.*

At last, as the Romans began to be driven back by the elephants and their horses, before they could get near the great beasts and started to panic and bolt, Pyrrhus seized his opportunity. As the Romans faltered, he launched a charge with his cavalry and routed the enemy with great slaughter. . . . The Romans lost nearly 15,000 men.

phalanx sometimes impaled the poor creatures. Also, a common anti-elephant tactic was to litter the field with sharp spikes. Pachyderms whose feet were mutilated by such spikes tended to fly out of control and sometimes smashed into the ranks of their own army. Eventually, the disadvantages of battle elephants came to outweigh the advantages. In short, over the course of two or three centuries, these beasts steadily lost their novelty and their use as weapons ceased.

In a very real way, the failure of the elephants was a symptom of a major inherent military weakness of this age of excess. In the long run, multitudes of mercenaries, giant siege engines, and monstrous beasts, though sometimes effective, proved unwieldy, heavy-handed, and/or inflexible. As the Hellenistic monarchs bickered, far to the west, in fertile Italy, a bright new star was rising. A more flexible, ultimately more lethal military system—that of Rome—was taking shape, a well-oiled fighting machine that would soon render Greek warfare obsolete.

CHAPTER FIVE

Oar, Sail, and Ram: Greek Warships and Their Crews

Throughout the Bronze, Archaic, Classical, and Hellenistic Ages, as Greek land warfare evolved and changed, naval warfare underwent its own development. One important wartime role played by ancient ships was to support land armies. Sometimes the ships ferried troops from one place to another; or they carried essential supplies, often moving along a coastline and keeping pace with the land troops, who stayed near the seacoast as they marched. Greek warships also engaged in naval battles.

Only a few literary descriptions of such encounters have survived, and most of these are not very detailed. But combined with wall and vase paintings, as well as fragments of actual warships discovered by archaeologists, they allow historians to piece together a general picture of Greek warships and their crews and tactics over the centuries.

Bronze Age Navies

Very little is known about Bronze Age Greek ships and how they were used. But there is no doubt that the Minoans and Mycenaeans had ships and that such vessels were essential to their control of the Aegean waterways. Thucydides wrote:

> Minos, according to tradition, was the first person to organize a navy. He controlled the greater part of what is now called the Hellenic [Aegean] Sea; he ruled over the Cyclades [the island group north of Crete], in most of which he founded the first colonies. . . . And it is reasonable to suppose that he did his best to put down piracy in order to secure his own revenues.[40]

King Minos was a renowned ruler of Crete in Greek mythology. His legendary character and exploits probably represent a garbled memory of Minoan rulers in general, for there is no doubt that the Minoans had numerous ships and traded widely in the Aegean and other parts of the Mediterranean.

Some evidence suggests that when the Mycenaeans eventually took over the Minoan sphere in the late Bronze Age, the Mycenaeans came to engage more in piracy than trade. The Greek expedition to Troy described in Homer's *Iliad* may well be a memory of such pirate raids. Thucydides's own sources contain similar memories. "In these early times," he wrote, as communication by sea became easier, piracy became a common profession both among the Greeks and among the barbarians [non-Greeks] who lived on the coast and in the islands. The leading pirates were powerful men, acting both out of self-interest and in order to support the weak among their own peo-

A modern replica of an early Greek sailing vessel similar to the kind used by the heroes Odysseus and Jason in Greek mythology.

ple. They would descend upon cities which were unprotected by walls . . . and by plundering such places they would gain most of their livelihood. At this time such a profession, so far from being regarded as disgraceful, was considered quite honorable.[41]

The raids described here, as well as the attack on Troy, involved ships carrying and disembarking land warriors. What about warfare between the ships themselves? Among the clues showing that such battles did occur is a surviving segment of a wall fresco found on the Aegean island of Thera (the southernmost of the Cyclades, about seventy miles north of Crete). It depicts the conclusion of a naval battle fought between Aegean (presumably Mycenaean) warriors and non-Aegeans. The Aegeans are recognizable by their attire and equipment; their opponents are nude and carry non-Aegean shields. These opponents are flailing around and drowning, while the Aegean warriors march along on land, suggesting that the fresco commemorates an Aegean victory. That the painting shows a naval battle rather than a shipwreck is proven by a representation of a grappling-iron. This device, which fighters on one ship used to hook and hold fast an enemy ship, has been a common feature of naval warfare throughout the ages.

Who were these opponents the Bronze Age Greeks fought at sea? They may have been non-Greek pirates. Or they may have been Egyptians, though if they were, the battle depicted would likely have occurred in Egyptian rather than Aegean waters. Some graphic stone bas-reliefs found at

Thebes, in Egypt, show a naval battle fought on Egypt's northern coast by the pharaoh Ramses III against invaders, some of whom may have been Mycenaean Greeks. Unfortunately, the evidence for sea battles between Bronze Age Greeks and Egyptians, as well as the nature of Bronze Age warships and their crews, remains scant and inconclusive.

The Pentekonter

Not until the Archaic Age does the surviving evidence begin to give a clearer picture of Greek ships and their use in warfare. Homer, who likely lived in the late eighth century B.C., provides some valuable descriptions of ships, especially in his *Odyssey*. These are almost certainly the ships of his own day, not Bronze Age vessels. Some important details of their appearance are found in the scene in which a goddess helps the hero Odysseus construct one:

First, she gave him a great ax of bronze. . . . Next she handed him an adze [a cutting tool with a curved blade for shaping wood] of polished metal. . . . When she had shown him the place where the trees were tallest . . . Odysseus began to cut the timbers down. . . . Twenty trees in all he felled, and lopped their branches with his ax; then he trimmed them in a workmanlike manner. . . . With augers [drills] he drilled through all his planks, cut them to fit across each other, and fixed this flooring together by means of dowels [small wooden cylinders] driven through the interlocking joints. . . . He next

An ancient Greek bireme, pictured here, had two banks of rowers in addition to its sail, giving it more speed than a pentekonter.

put up the decking, which he fitted to [wooden] ribs at short intervals. . . . He made a mast to go in the boat, with a yardarm [crosspiece to hold the sail] fitted to it; and a steering oar, too, to keep her on her course.[42]

This ship Odysseus built was small but had most of the basic features of larger vessels then in use. The main warship in the era was the pentekonter, with fifty rowers who all sat on the same level, or bank, twenty-five on each side. Homer calls these ships "hollow," indicating that they lacked decks, like modern dories and racing shells. At least there was no *main* deck. Some ancient paintings show small platforms set up at the bow (front) for the captain and stern (rear) for the helmsman to stand on.

Very little room existed for storage on such a vessel; it was so cramped, in fact, that sailors had to sleep at their oars. Thus, the pentekonter was impractical for long voyages at sea; and skippers stuck mainly to shorelines or hopped from one island to the next. Indeed, Homer and other ancient authors frequently described crews beaching their vessels each night and landing often to search for food and other supplies.

When it came time to fight, the crew lowered the sail and mast and relied solely on oar-power. Ancient paintings show pentekonters with bronze beaks, or rams, projecting from the bows near the waterline. So the principal offensive tactic was likely to build up some speed and attempt to ram and sink an enemy vessel. Hand-to-hand fighting was probably rare in this period; if and when it occurred, some of the rowers may have grabbed swords and doubled as marines (fighters). In any case, the era of the pentekonter probably saw few naval engagements, and those that did occur were likely small. These ships were light, fragile, and not very maneuverable; and strenuous battle tactics would have been extremely dangerous for both ship and crew.

The Advent of the Trireme

This situation steadily began to change after Homer's time, however. About 700 B.C. or so, the bireme appeared. With two banks of oars, it was shorter, more powerful, and more maneuverable than the pentekonter. An even more revolutionary change occurred in the sixth century B.C. with the addition of a third bank of oars, producing the trireme (*trieres*), which re-

mained the principal Greek warship for some time to come.

A trireme was generally about 130 feet long, 18 feet wide, and carried a crew of about 200. In an Athenian trireme (for which the best evidence has survived), this included 170 rowers. They were not slaves, as sometimes portrayed in Hollywood movies, but highly trained professionals recruited mainly from Athens's lower classes (although some were likely mercenaries). The crew also included a flute player who kept time for the rowers, a fighting force of ten hoplite marines (*epibatai*) and four archers, and fifteen deckhands. One of the latter, the helmsman (*kubernetes*), was usually more experienced and knowledgeable about naval matters than anyone else on board.

BEACHED SHIPS CAPTURED BY THE ENEMY

The fact that triremes had to be beached each day to allow their crews to rest and look for food left them vulnerable to enemy attack. This is how the Athenians lost the pivotal battle of Aegospotami in 405 B.C. and with it the long Peloponnesian War against Sparta and its allies. Xenophon describes the incident in this excerpt from his Hellenica.

Lysander [the Spartan commander] instructed some of his fastest ships to follow the Athenians and, when they had disembarked, to observe what they were doing. . . . [The Spartans followed for four days and saw that each day] the Athenians moored on an open shore with no city behind them and got their supplies from [a distance of] two miles

away from their ships. . . . On the fifth day . . . Lysander gave special instructions [to his men]. . . . As soon as they saw that the Athenians had disembarked and had scattered in various directions . . . they were to sail back and to signal [him]. . . . These orders were carried out and . . . Lysander ordered the fleet to sail [for the beaches] at full speed. . . . When Conon [the Athenian commander] saw that the enemy were attacking, he signaled to the Athenians to hurry back as fast as they could to their ships. But they were scattered in all directions. . . . Conon himself in his own ship and seven others . . . did get to sea fully manned . . . [but] all the rest were captured by Lysander on land. He also rounded up nearly all the crews.

This photo taken from the top of the mast of a reconstructed Greek ship of the Archaic Age shows the benches for the rowers, as described by Homer.

The captain, or trierarch (*trierarchos*), was most often a wealthy individual fulfilling his duty to the state. Each year a few hundred wealthy Athenians were each called on to outfit and maintain one trireme for the coming season. The state provided the ship and paid the rowers; the trierarch supplied much of the equipment, paid the officers, bore the cost of any repairs, and commanded the ship (al-though if a novice, he probably heavily relied on the advice of the veteran helms-man).[43]

Like pentekonters, triremes lacked eat-ing and sleeping facilities, which meant that they still had to be beached once a day and were therefore impractical for long-term naval strategy. Describing the tactics of an Athenian admiral, Xenophon wrote:

When his force [of ships] was just ready to take the morning or evening meal, he would order the leading ships of the column to come about . . . and form into line . . . facing the land, and at a signal make them race to the shore. And it was something really to be proud of to be the first to get water or whatever else was wanted and to be the first to get one's meal.[44]

F.E. Adcock lists some of the trireme's other disadvantages for use in warfare:

They were blind at night and had poor communications at sea. They lay low in the water, and even if they were proceeding under sail they had no tall masts to help them watch out for the enemy or signal to each other. When they were operating as fighting fleets and nothing else, they carried too few marines to secure a landing on a hostile coast without serious risk. They might, in favorable conditions, block a harbor, but they could not blockade a long coastline. . . . The ships themselves rapidly deteriorated unless

THE SLAUGHTER AT SALAMIS

In his play The Persians, *first produced in 472 B.C., the Athenian playwright Aeschylus, who fought in the sea battle at Salamis, describes how Greek sailors and hoplites, after gaining the advantage, slaughtered the terrified enemy by the thousands. In this excerpt (from Philip Vellacott's translation), a messenger tells the Persian queen mother:*

Then from the Greek ships rose like a song of joy the piercing battle-cry, and from the island crags echoed an answering shout. The Persians knew their error; fear gripped every man. They were no fugitives who sang that terrifying paean [battle hymn], but Greeks charging with courageous hearts to battle. . . . At once ship into ship battered its brazen beak. A Greek ship charged first, and chopped off the whole stern of a Persian galley. Then charge followed charge on every side. At first by its huge impetus our fleet withstood them. But soon, in that narrow space, our ships were jammed in hundreds; none could help another. They rammed each other with their prows of bronze; and some were stripped of every oar. Meanwhile the enemy came round us in a ring and charged. Our vessels heeled over; the sea was hidden, carpeted with wrecks and dead men; all the shores and reefs were full of dead. Then every ship we had broke rank and rowed for life. The Greeks seized fragments of wrecks and broken oars and hacked and stabbed at our men swimming in the sea. . . . The whole sea was one din of shrieks and dying groans, till night and darkness hid the scene. . . . Never before in one day died so vast a company of men.

they were well housed when not on active service, and they had much to fear from bad weather when they were.[45]

Triremes in Battle

Naval strategy for triremes was therefore of a short-term nature, mainly concerned with how to win an individual battle as quickly and safely as possible. The basic strategy continued to emphasize ramming runs to sink enemy ships. Various tactics developed to outmaneuver opposing vessels and make it easier to ram them, among them the *periplus,* in which an attacking fleet tried to outflank an enemy fleet. If the attackers succeeded in

Greek warships defeat the Persian armada at Salamis in 480 B.C. Unable to maneuver well in the narrow strait, the Persian vessels were easy prey to Greek ramming runs.

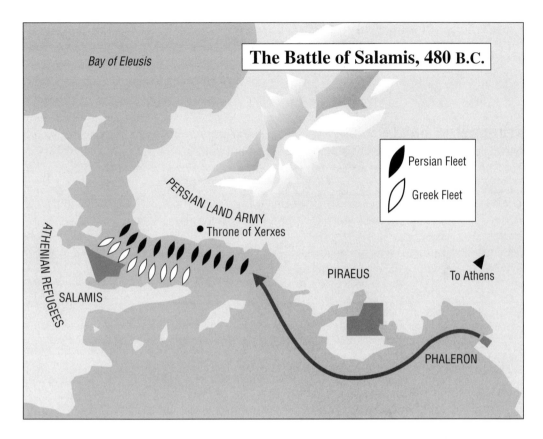

The Battle of Salamis, 480 B.C.

Bay of Eleusis

Persian Fleet

Greek Fleet

PERSIAN LAND ARMY
● Throne of Xerxes

ATHENIAN REFUGEES

SALAMIS

PIRAEUS

To Athens

PHALERON

enveloping the sides of the opposing fleet, they could ram the exposed sides of the outer ships in the enemy's line. Another common maneuver was the *diekplus,* described by Lionel Casson, a noted authority on ancient naval warfare:

In battle, opponents generally faced each other in two long lines. The one carrying out the *diekplus* would at a given signal dash forward so suddenly and swiftly that his ships were able to row through the enemy's line before the latter was able to take countermeasures, wheel [around] when through [the line], and ram the unprotected quarters or sterns [of the enemy's ships]. It was a deadly maneuver, but it demanded the utmost in coordination, response to command, and cleanness of execution; only fast ships and finely trained crews, taught to work in unison, could carry it out successfully.[46]

In another naval battle tactic, a ship attacked an enemy vessel at an angle, shearing off most of its oars on one side and thereby rendering it helpless; a second attacker, stationed directly behind the first, then moved in for the killing ramming run. Still another offensive maneuver was to use grappling hooks or ropes to lock

RECONSTRUCTING A GIANT WARSHIP

In this tract from Greek and Roman Naval Warfare, *military historian William L. Rodgers attempts to reconstruct the details of a "sixteen," one of the monstrous Greek warships built in Hellenistic times.*

We assume a crew of 100 officers, seamen, and mechanics, 440 soldiers, and 800 rowers with 10 days' water, food, and fire wood. Assume also 20 tons for mechanical artillery and hurling stones, making a total weight of 237 tons. With hull and equipment of 63 percent of the load displacement, the latter [i.e., the displacement in the water] will be 640 tons. Assume two levels of 25 oars on each side on each level. . . . For the linear dimensions, assume a 38 foot beam between tholepins [oarlocks], and 30 feet at the water line, which will give good stability with a large number of men moving freely on the upper deck. For such a wide ship, a suitable sail area would be 1.25 times the rectangle about the water line, or 6,750 square feet, divided among 2 or 3 masts. . . . The deck area of the two principal decks would be about 8,700 square feet, enough for quartering 1,300 men. . . . The rest would find room to sleep on the raised flooring for the rowers. Presumably the upper deck was protected at night by a heavy awning and there were weather curtains along its sides, as in the Middle Ages. This great ship differs in speed little from a trireme, but carries soldiers and heavy artillery. The cost was far too great for any but a great prince and was a rarity even for such.

two ships together; the marines from one vessel then boarded the other and fought hand to hand.

Ramming and boarding were both used to tremendous effect by the Greeks in the first major sea battle ever recorded in any detail. It took place in 480 B.C. in the strait between the Greek mainland and the island of Salamis, where the Greeks met a larger fleet of Persian warships. Hemmed inside the narrow waterway, the Persian vessels became trapped and had trouble maneuvering. When the Greek fleet attacked, the Persian galleys in the front row slowed almost to a halt; and soon the galleys in the rear rows began piling up on those in the front. This allowed the Greeks to launch ramming runs almost at will. The Athenian play-wright Aeschylus, who fought at Salamis, recalled: "At once ship into ship battered its brazen beak. A Greek ship charged first, and chopped off the whole stern of a Persian galley. Then charge followed charge on every side."[47] The immobility of the trapped Persian ships must have allowed for considerable hand-to-hand fighting, while Greek sailors and marines dispatched enemy seamen struggling in the water. "The Greeks seized fragments of wrecks and broken oars," according to Aeschylus, "and hacked and stabbed at [the Persian] men swimming in the sea."[48] The slaughter was so great and the victory so decisive that it gave the Greeks effective naval superiority over the eastern Mediterranean sphere for centuries to come.

Hellenistic Warships and Sea Battles

In the fourth century B.C. and on into Hellenistic times, larger warships appeared. Triremes were sometimes called "threes" in reference to their three oar banks. The newer warships included "fours," "fives," "sixes," and so on, reaching as large as "sixteens" by the start of the third century B.C. and "forties" by the close of that century. Clearly, these larger numbers cannot have denoted the number of oar banks. Even if a ship with sixteen banks of oars could have been built, it would have been prohibitively expensive to maintain and so top-heavy and unmaneuverable as to be useless in warfare.

It is more likely that the numbers in question referred to how many men worked an oar, multiplied by the number of oar banks. Take, for example, the quadrireme and quinquereme, the latter of which became very common in naval warfare in succeeding centuries. Both were somewhat larger than a trireme. A quadrireme, or "four," appears to have had two banks of oars, with two men to each oar. The quinquereme, or "five," took this design a step further, so that it had three oar banks, the top two having two rowers to an oar and the bottom one

A modern drawing depicts a large Hellenistic warship featuring a battle tower erected near the bow and more than a hundred fighters crowding the main deck.

having one man to an oar. (The quinquereme was up to 120 feet long and carried some 270 rowers, 30 crewmen, and from 40 to 120 marines.) A "sixteen" was therefore likely a two-banked ship with eight rowers per oar. It was probably a large vessel with a wide deck designed to carry large numbers of troops, siege artillery, and so forth.

In fact, the advent of these larger warships signaled a transition from naval warfare consisting primarily of ramming runs to a strategy that also included massed artillery barrages and other features of land warfare. A typical navy of the Hellenistic period had some triremes for swift maneuvers and ramming, along with many larger ships for launching missile attacks and transferring large squads of troops onto enemy decks. An example is the great battle fought off the coast of Cyprus in 307 B.C. by the fleets of two of the leading Successors—Demetrius and Ptolemy. According to Diodorus:

> The two fleets being about 600 yards apart, Demetrius gave the signal to engage. . . . Ptolemy did the same and the two fleets closed quickly with each other. . . . The engagement opened with archery and stones and darts from the catapults, and many were wounded during the approach. Then contact was made . . . and the men on deck fell on [attacked] the enemy with spears. The first shock was violent, some ships had their oars swept from their sides and remained motionless . . . and in the meantime the soldiers attacked each other hand-to-hand. . . . The ships being held in contact became so many fields of battle with the boarders leaping to the enemy's decks.[49]

The last time a Greek ruler led warships into battle was in 31 B.C., when Ptolemy's descendant, Cleopatra VII (and her Roman lover Mark Antony), faced off against the Romans at Actium (in western Greece). Cleopatra lost. And for the rest of ancient times, naval warfare played only an occasional and minor role in Western warfare. Long before Actium, the Romans had managed to neutralize the Greeks on land. And after it, no other European power possessed a navy capable of challenging Rome.

CHAPTER SIX

The Cost of Disunity: Greek Armies Fall to Roman Steel

Eventually, the Greeks lost their pre-eminent position of power and prestige in the eastern Mediterranean. Their fall had two major causes, the first one military and the other political. The Greek military decline stemmed in large part from the Hellenistic arms race in which leaders constantly tried to outspend one another. Buying mercenaries and ever-larger weapons was in the end a poor substitute for the national interest, patriotism, and courage of local citizens, factors that had made hoplite armies consistently successful. The "infatuation with gigantism," Victor Hanson suggests, "was more a reflection of imperial prestige . . . than a response to military challenge. . . . The Successor generals simplistically tried to match the lost tactical skill of Alexander with purchased manpower and brute force of arms."[50]

The political dimension in the Greeks' decline—persistent disunity—went hand in hand with the military aspect, as constant rivalry consumed the Hellenistic monarchs as much as imperial prestige. The problem long predated these rulers, however. Indeed, such rivalries had been a fact of Greek life for centuries. As for why the Greeks so stubbornly failed to unite, some historians have suggested that Greece's geography played a major role. Because it is riddled by rugged mountains and numerous islands, physically it is naturally divided into many small regions. According to this view, the localized nature of these regions promoted the growth of not only small city-states, but also a fierce spirit of independence. Other scholars point to the Greeks' intense devotion to competition. "The Greeks were one of the most competitive peoples in history," scholar Robert J. Littman writes.

Greek athletes compete in the Panathenaic Games, held very four years in Athens. The Greeks were naturally competitive, which contributed to their disunity.

Everything was made into a contest, from athletics to the great drama festivals. . . . Competition was formalized in the great *agones,* public festivals at which competitors contended. . . . Much of the competition, however, was nonproductive. . . . The Greeks regarded any kind of defeat as disgraceful, regardless of circumstances. . . . Egoism, the need to excel, to gain honor and glory at the expense of others, helped to produce a society incapable of unity. The individual would not risk sacrificing himself for the city-state, nor the city-state for the welfare of Greece.[51]

Whatever its cause, this continued disunity led the Greeks to fight among themselves almost incessantly. These conflicts culminated in the disastrous Peloponnesian War (431–404 B.C.), which engulfed and exhausted most of the Greek world and signaled the beginning of the decline of Greek power and independence in the Mediterranean. More bickering among the city-states in the fourth century B.C. led to their eclipse by Philip and Alexander; and the quarrels among the Hellenistic realms further reinforced Greek disunity, finally leaving the Greek world terribly war-weary and vulnerable to attack by an outside power.

That power, of course, turned out to be Rome, master of the Italian peninsula. In the second and first centuries B.C., the Romans picked off the Greek states one by one and absorbed them into their expanding empire. It was Rome, therefore, and not Greece, that subsequently went on to unite the whole Mediterranean world into a vast commonwealth administered by one central government. At the same time, however, Rome adopted many Greek ideas, including military ones, and eventually passed them on to later Western cultures.

The First Greco-Roman Military Encounters

Could Rome's conquest of Greece and the latter's fall have been prevented? Perhaps, but only if the Greeks had recognized the military threat Rome posed early enough and then banded together to deal with it. As it was, they failed to recognize the danger until it was too late and even then they remained disunited.

This pattern of arrogance, lack of foresight, and denial is apparent in the first tentative military encounters between Greeks and Romans. In the early third century B.C., as the Hellenistic kings continued to squabble, one of them decided to test himself against the growing power of Rome. Pyrrhus of Epirus, who had introduced the idea of mounting armored towers on the backs of battle elephants, received an urgent plea for aid. It came from Tarentum, the most prosperous and important of the Greek cities that had for several centuries dotted southern Italy.[52] The Tarentines had recently sunk a small fleet of Roman ships that had violated their territorial waters; and they feared that Rome would retaliate by sending its land army against them.

Pyrrhus answered this call for help. But in crossing to Italy with his army in the spring of 280 B.C., he was likely motivated by more than just sympathy for his fellow Greeks. Plutarch attributes the following remarks to him:

> If we can conquer the Romans, there is no other Greek or barbarian [non-Greek] city which is a match for us. We shall straightaway become the masters of the whole of Italy. . . . After Italy, [we will take] Sicily, of course. . . . We can make it the spring-board for much greater enterprises.[53]

Driven by these dreams of conquest, Pyrrhus met the Romans in battle at Heraclea, not far from Tarentum. This was the encounter in which his elephants frightened the Roman horsemen and clinched his victory. But it was a costly win; for the Romans showed themselves to be stubborn and courageous fighters and slew some four thousand of Pyrrhus's men, over a sixth of his army. He fought the Romans again the following year at Ausculum, in southeastern Italy, and won again. But this

An ancient bust of Pyrrhus, who narrowly defeated the Romans at great cost to his own army.

81

Pyrrhus's troops and elephants meet the Roman legions head on at Ausculum, in southern Italy. The Greeks won but the margin of victory was very narrow.

time his losses were so great that he is said to have joked: "One more victory like that over the Romans will destroy us completely!"[54] Ever since, an excessively costly win has been called a "Pyrrhic victory."

After fighting still another costly battle against the Romans in 275 B.C., Pyrrhus decided to cut his losses and return to Epirus. The failure of his Italian adventure had extremely ominous overtones; the fact that he, one of the greatest Greek generals of his day, could not decisively defeat the Romans did not bode well for Greece's future.

Unfortunately for Pyrrhus and his fellow Greek generals, they did not grasp an important underlying reason for the Romans' ability to resist the onslaught of a large Greek army. The Romans had learned much from the Greeks over the years. In particular, they had managed to avoid the disunity and political and financial corruption displayed by the Hellenistic states. Moreover, Roman soldiers of this period were independent farmers, members of agrarian militias that hearkened back to those of Archaic and Classical Greece. These militias, Hanson asserts, "with their emphasis on group solidarity, patriotism, and belief in a superior culture," were in a sense "more Greek than the Hellenistic military dynasties they met." By contrast, the armies of Alexander's Successors "had become every bit as despotic, top-heavy, and corrupt as the old Persian imperial armies, whom the Greeks had conquered almost two centuries earlier."[55]

The Greek Phalanx Compared to the Roman Legion

Having learned nothing from Pyrrhus's encounters with Rome, the Greeks proceeded to ignore more handwriting on the wall regarding the growing threat of the Roman military. Only eleven years after Pyrrhus had vacated Italy, Rome launched the first of three devastating conflicts (the so-called Punic Wars) against the maritime empire of Carthage, centered in Tunisia, in North Africa. The First Punic War (264–241 B.C.) proved to be the most destructive conflict the world had yet seen. Decisive victory gave Rome control over the large island of Sicily and allowed it to begin building an overseas empire.

The Second Punic War (218–202 B.C.) soon followed. In this truly stupendous conflict, Greeks and Romans opposed each other once more (though their actual contact on the battlefield was limited). Philip V, king of the Hellenistic kingdom

---

STRENGTHS AND WEAKNESSES OF THE PHALANX

In this excerpt from his Histories, *from a section titled "On the Phalanx," Polybius discusses some of the strengths of the Macedonian phalanx in use in his own day and also some of its weaknesses.*

There are a number of factors which make it easy to understand that so long as the phalanx retains its characteristic form and strength, nothing can withstand its charge or resist it face to face. When the phalanx is closed up for action, each man with his arms [weapons] occupies a space of three feet. . . . The pike will protect fifteen feet in front of the body of each hoplite when he advances against the enemy grasping it with both hands. . . . It follows that each man in the front rank will have the points of five pikes extending in front of him, each point being three feet ahead of the one behind. From these facts we can easily picture the nature and the tremendous power of a charge by the whole phalanx, when it advances sixteen deep with leveled pikes. . . . What then is the factor which enables the Ro-

mans to win the battle and causes those who use the phalanx to fail? The answer is that in war the times and places for action are unlimited, whereas the phalanx requires one time and one type of ground only in order to produce its peculiar effect. . . . It is generally admitted that its use requires flat and level ground which is unencumbered by any obstacles such as ditches, gullies . . . and water-courses. . . . It is almost impossible, or at any rate exceedingly rare, to find a stretch of country of say two or three miles or more which contains no obstacles of this kind. . . . The Romans do not attempt to make their line numerically equal to the enemy's, nor do they expose the whole strength of the legions to a frontal attack by the phalanx. Instead, they keep part of the forces in reserve while the rest engage the enemy. . . . [Such] reserves can occupy the space the phalanx has vacated [while moving forward], and . . . can fall upon it from flank [side] and rear. . . . Does it not follow that the difference between these two [military] systems is enormous?

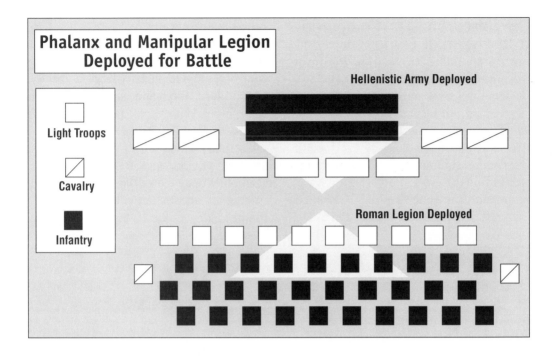

Phalanx and Manipular Legion Deployed for Battle

Light Troops

Cavalry

Infantry

Hellenistic Army Deployed

Roman Legion Deployed

of Macedonia, made the mistake of allying himself with the ultimate loser—Carthage. (The Romans later referred to their involvement with him as the First Macedonian War, a subconflict of the greater war with Carthage.) In its victory, Rome gained control of almost all the shores of the western Mediterranean. And less than two years after signing the treaty with Carthage, the Romans were ready to punish Philip for his interference in their affairs. In this way Rome, which had recently become master of the western Mediterranean sphere, now turned its attention to the Greek states in the sea's eastern sphere.

Largely because these states remained disunited, their fates were virtually sealed. The so-called Second Macedonian War (200–197 B.C.) was noteworthy because it pitted the Mediterranean world's two most prestigious and feared military systems against each other. (Though Pyrrhus's battles with Rome had done the same, they had ended in a draw, more or less, so they were seen as inconclusive.) In contrast with the main offensive weapon of the Greek armies—the Macedonian phalanx—Roman armies then consisted of legions, groups of about 4,500 to 5,000 soldiers. On the battlefield each legion broke down into smaller units called maniples, having from 60 to 120 men each. The maniples were arranged into lines with open spaces between both the maniples and the lines. This allowed individual units to move back and forth with ease, permitting tired troops to fall back and rest while fresh ones pressed forward into the fray. When need dictated, various-sized contingents of maniples could also separate from the army's main body and fight on their own. Over time Roman generals also came to arrange maniples and other battlefield units into strategic patterns, such as huge diagonal lines, wedges, and so on.

In short, each individual maniple or group of maniples was less formidable than a large Greek phalanx. Yet the Roman units could move back, forward, and around quickly at a commander's order, giving the Roman army a degree of flexi-bility that the stiff, monolithic phalanx lacked. Polybius had pointed out that nothing could withstand the frontal attack of a Macedonian phalanx as long as it retained its shape and strength. "What then," he asked, "is the factor which enables the Romans to win the battle and causes those who use the phalanx to fail?"[56] The answer was that the phalanx could operate effectively only on flat ground unencumbered by obstacles; when

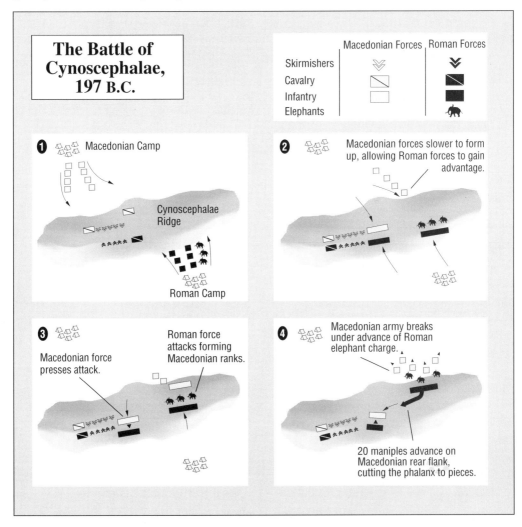

The Battle of Cynoscephalae, 197 B.C.

	Macedonian Forces	Roman Forces
Skirmishers		
Cavalry		
Infantry		
Elephants		

1 Macedonian Camp
Cynoscephalae Ridge
Roman Camp

2 Macedonian forces slower to form up, allowing Roman forces to gain advantage.

3 Macedonian force presses attack.
Roman force attacks forming Macedonian ranks.

4 Macedonian army breaks under advance of Roman elephant charge.
20 maniples advance on Macedonian rear flank, cutting the phalanx to pieces.

PERSEUS'S PHALANX FALLS TO PIECES

The pivotal battle of Pydna, fought in 168 B.C. between the Macedonians under King Perseus and the Romans under Aemilius Paulus, showed the superior flexibility of the Roman army over the rigid phalanx. Here is part of Plutarch's description of the battle, from his biography of Aemilius (John Dryden's translation).

The conflict grew very fierce and the slaughter terrible on both sides. For [some of the Romans] endeavored to cut the [Greek pikemen's] spears asunder with their swords, or to beat them back with their shields . . . and on the other side, the Macedonians held their long *sarissas* in both hands, and pierced those [Romans] who came in their way right through their armor, shield or cuirass being unable to resist the force of that weapon. . . . Nevertheless, the unevenness of the ground would not permit [the phalanx to keep] a widely extended front . . . [and] have their shields everywhere joined. And Aemilius perceived that there were a great many breaches in the Macedonian phalanx. . . . [So he quickly] broke up his men into their [maniples] and ordered them to move into the intervals and openings of the enemy's formation . . . and no sooner had they entered the spaces and separated their enemies, but they charged them, some on their sides where they were naked and exposed, and others . . . [from] behind, and thus destroyed the force of the phalanx. . . . Now, fighting man to man or in small parties, the Macedonians struck in vain with their little swords on [the Romans'] firm, long shields, while their own small shields were not able to sustain the weight and force of the Roman swords, which pierced through their armor right to their bodies. They turned . . . and fled. . . . It is said that there fell 25,000 [Macedonians]; of the Romans, a hundred.

it was forced to fight on uneven ground or an enemy unexpectedly attacked it from the rear, it was seriously vulnerable. Also, it was a single, solid, inflexible mass of soldiers whose separate lines and files were neither intended nor trained to act independently. "Whereas," Polybius wrote, "the Roman formation is highly flexible. Every Roman soldier, once he . . . goes into action, can adapt himself equally well to any place or time and meet an attack from any quarter."[57]

Sooner or later, the more flexible Roman system was bound to exploit these weaknesses. As military historian Lawrence Keppie aptly puts it, "The Macedonians and Greeks, who . . . carried the phalanx to extremes of regimentation and automation, fossilized the very instrument of their former success, to their eventual downfall."[58]

The Demise of the Phalanx

The first crucial battle that foreshadowed that downfall took place in 197 B.C. at Cynoscephalae ("Dog's Head"), a steep hill in central Greece. The outcome of this pivotal engagement of the Second Macedonian War fully confirmed Polybius's astute analysis and showed that the Greek system, which had largely dominated Mediterranean land warfare for centuries, had become outmoded. The Macedonians were led by their king, Philip V, while the Roman commander was Titus Quinctius Flamininus. The two armies approached the hill and made camp, the Macedonians to the north, the Romans to the south.

The next morning each commander, unaware of the enemy's close proximity (mainly because fog blanketed the area) sent out a small covering force of skirmishers and horsemen to take control of the hill. At the summit these forces ran into each other, a fight ensued, and in the coming hours it steadily escalated. "As

the mist was clearing," Peter Connolly writes,

both sides now decided to bring up the rest of their forces. The Romans were nearer to the pass and managed to deploy their forces while Philip was still bringing up his. Only his right wing [i.e., the right half of his phalanx] had reached the top. . . . [His] cavalry and light-armed [troops], who were already engaged [with the Romans], were withdrawn and formed up on the right [of the phalanx]. Flamininus placed the elephants

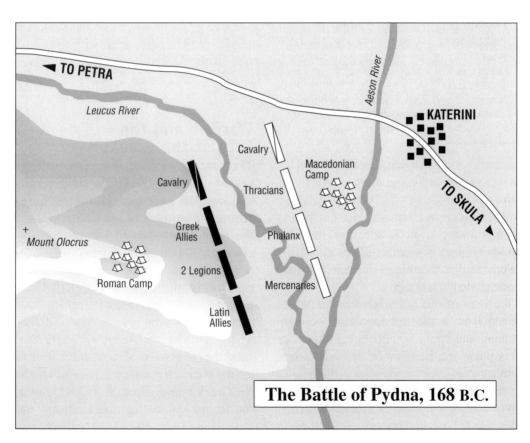

The Battle of Pydna, 168 B.C.

which were with his army in front of his right wing, told his troops there to stand fast, and advanced with his left wing. Philip . . . ordered [the members of] his phalanx to lower their spears and charge. . . . The charge of the phalanx drove the legionaries back down the slope. Flamininus, seeing the imminent destruction of his left wing, threw himself at the head of the right wing and charged the Macedonian left wing, which was still forming up. The half-assembled Macedonian line crumbled before the onslaught of the elephants. . . . One of the tribunes [in the Roman right wing], seizing the initiative, took 20 maniples . . . faced about, and charged . . . into the rear of the Macedonian right wing. The action was decisive; the phalanx, unable to turn, was cut to pieces. The Romans followed up their victory, cutting down the Macedonians where they stood, even though they raised their pikes to surrender.[59]

The bloated Greek casualty lists helped to reinforce the truth of the phalanx's demise. Philip's losses included some 8,000 killed and 5,000 captured, while Flamininus lost only 700 men.

The results of the Greco-Roman battles and wars in the ensuing decades were hauntingly similar. A major highlight occurred in the summer of 168 B.C. when Philip's son, Perseus, challenged Rome in the Third Macedonian War (171–168 B.C.). At Pydna (in northern Greece), Perseus's phalanx clashed with a Roman army commanded by Aemilius Paulus. The Greek pikemen acquitted themselves well at first. But soon Aemelius saw that the somewhat uneven ground had caused gaps to open in the phalanx, and he immediately sent small mobile units into these gaps. Within minutes the Greek formation had splintered into many small groups, which the Roman troops surrounded. "Now, fighting man to man or in small parties," wrote Plutarch, "the Macedonians struck in vain with their little swords on [the Romans'] firm, long shields, while their own small shields were not able to sustain the weight and force of the Roman swords, which pierced through their armor right to their bodies."[60]

Once again the Greek phalanx was cut to pieces. (The war ended with the abolition of the Macedonian kingdom; Rome annexed the area as a new province in 148 B.C.)

Warfare and the Fate of the Greeks

These and other similar Roman victories rapidly rendered the Greek military system obsolete and made possible Rome's absorption of most of the Greek lands in the coming decades. In 146 B.C., after a courageous but futile military resistance by a federation of southern Greek cities, the Romans brutally destroyed the once great city of Corinth as an object lesson to other Greeks who might dare to rebel. That federation, the Achaean League, had seen the wisdom of Greek unity. But its efforts proved too little and too late to save the Greek world. Back in 213 B.C., when the Romans were fighting Carthage and positioning themselves for Mediterranean

A CALL FOR GREEK UNITY

In 213 B.C. a Greek orator, Agelaus of Aetolia, recognized the potential danger Rome's rising power posed to the Greeks and delivered the following prophetic warning (preserved by the second-century B.C. Greek historian Polybius in his Histories*). Unfortunately for Greece, Agelaus's words were largely ignored.*

It would be best of all if the Greeks never went to war with one another, if they could regard it as the greatest gift of the gods for them to speak with one voice, and could join hands like men who are crossing a river; in this way they could unite to repulse the incursions of the barbarians [non-Greeks] and to preserve themselves and their cities. But if we have no hope of achieving such a degree of unity for the whole of the country, let me impress on you how important it is at least for the present that we should consult one another and remain on our guard, in view of the huge armies which have been mobilized, and vast scale of the war [the Second Punic War] which is now being waged in the west. For it must already be obvious to all those who pay even the slightest attention to affairs of state that whether the Carthaginians defeat the Romans or the Romans the Carthaginians, the victors will by no means be satisfied with the sovereignty of Italy and Sicily, but will come here, and will advance both their forces and their ambitions beyond the bounds of justice.

mastery, a Greek orator, Agelaus of Aetolia, had recognized the potential danger and warned:

It would be best of all if the Greeks never went to war with one another, if they could regard it as the greatest gift of the gods for them to speak with one voice, and could join hands like men who are crossing a river; in this way they could unite to repulse the incursions of the barbarians and to preserve themselves and their cities.[61]

At the time the Hellenistic world's great powers could have and certainly should have joined forces, as Agelaus urged, and presented a united front against the Roman threat. But his warning went largely unheeded. Though the Romans subsequently passed Greece's cultural legacy on to later ages, ensuring its survival, Greece became subservient to Rome; and nearly two thousand years would pass before the world would see the emergence of a true nation of Greece. This is but one example of how warfare, weapons, and their wise and effective use can profoundly affect the fate of an entire people.

Notes

Introduction: The Greek Way of War and Its Legacy in the West

1. Plato, *Laws,* in *Great Books of the Western World,* Vol. 7, trans. Benjamin Jowett. Chicago: Encyclopaedia Britannica, 1952, p. 641.

2. Victor D. Hanson, *The Wars of the Ancient Greeks and Their Invention of Western Military Culture.* London: Cassell, 1999, pp. 19–20.

3. Hanson, *Wars of the Ancient Greeks,* p. 22.

4. Hanson, *Wars of the Ancient Greeks,* p. 24.

5. F.E. Adcock, *The Greek and Macedonian Art of War.* Berkeley: University of California Press, 1957, pp. 7–8.

Chapter 1: Bronze Swords and Charging Chariots: Early Greek Warfare

6. C.M. Bowra, *Classical Greece.* New York: Time-Life, 1965, pp. 31–32.

7. Peter Connolly, *The Legend of Odysseus.* New York: Oxford University Press, 1986, p. 33.

8. Robert Drews, *The End of the Bronze Age: Changes in Warfare and the Catastrophe ca. 1200 B.C.* Princeton: Princeton University Press, 1993, pp. 127–29.

9. Drews, *End of the Bronze Age,* p. 97.

10. John Lazenby, "Hoplite Warfare," in Sir John Hackett, ed., *Warfare in the Ancient World,* New York: Facts On File, 1989, p. 54.

11. Hanson, *Wars of the Ancient Greeks,* pp. 40–41, 44.

Chapter 2: Farmers in Armor: The Development of the Hoplite Phalanx

12. Victor D. Hanson, *The Other Greeks: The Family Farm and the Agrarian Roots of Western Civilization.* New York: Simon and Schuster, 1995, p. 222.

13. Hanson, *Wars of the Ancient Greeks,* p. 48.

14. See Walter Donlon and James Thompson, "The Charge at Marathon," *Classical Journal,* vol. 71, 1976; and "The Charge at Marathon Again," *Classical Journal,* vol. 72, 1979.

15. John Warry, *Warfare in the Classical World.* Norman: University of Oklahoma Press, 1995, p. 35.

16. See Thucydides, *The Peloponnesian War,* published as *The Landmark Thucydides: A Comprehensive Guide to the Peloponnesian War,* Robert B. Strassler, ed., Richard Crawley, trans., New York: Simon and Schuster, 1996, pp. 166–67.

17. See Thucydides, *Landmark Thucydides,* p. 231.

18. Thucydides, *Landmark Thucydides,* p. 471.

19. Peter Connolly, *Greece and Rome at War.* London: Greenhill Books, 1998, pp. 37–38.

20. See Xenophon, *The Constitution of the Lakedaimonians,* in *Scripta Minora,* trans. E.C. Marchant. Cambridge, MA: Harvard University Press, 1993, pp. 171–75.

21. Warry, *Warfare,* p. 37.

22. Quoted in Kenneth J. Atchity, ed., *The Classical Greek Reader.* New York: Oxford University Press, 1996, p. 43.

23. Polybius, *Histories,* published as *Polybius: The Rise of the Roman Empire,* trans. Ian Scott-Kilvert. New York: Penguin, 1979, p. 509.

24. Xenophon, *Anabasis,* trans. W.H.D. Rouse. New York: New American Library, 1959, p. 38.

25. Herodotus, *The Histories,* trans. Aubrey de Sélincourt. New York: Penguin, 1972, pp. 445–46.

26. Hanson, *Wars of the Ancient Greeks,* p. 66.

27. Hanson, *Wars of the Ancient Greeks,* p. 105.

Chapter 3: Epaminondas to Alexander: A Revolution in Military Tactics

28. Connolly, *Greece and Rome at War,* p. 51.

29. Some modern scholars doubt that Philip acquired much, if any, important military information while in Thebes. See, for instance, J.R. Ellis, *Philip II and Macedonian Imperialism.* New York: Thames and Hudson, 1977, pp. 43–44. It stands to reason, however, that a young man of his intelligence and ambition, living in such close proximity with the leading generals of the day, would have attempted to learn as much as he could about their army.

30. Xenophon, *The Art of Horsemanship,* in *Scripta Minora,* p. 363.

31. Hanson, *Wars of the Ancient Greeks,* p. 150.

32. Plutarch, *Life of Pelopidas,* in *The Age of Alexander: Nine Greek Lives by Plutarch,* Trans. Ian Scott-Kilvert. New York: Penguin, 1973, pp. 85–86.

33. J.F.C. Fuller, *The Generalship of Alexander the Great.* New Brunswick, NJ: Rutgers University Press, 1960, p. 292.

34. Hanson, *Wars of the Ancient Greeks,* p. 188.

Chapter 4: Mercenaries and Siege Machines: War in the Hellenistic Age

35. Hanson, *Wars of the Ancient Greeks,* pp. 196–97.

36. Warry, *Warfare,* pp. 92–93.

37. Plutarch, *Life of Demetrius,* in *Age of Alexander,* p. 352.

38. Arrian, *Anabasis Alexandri,* published as *The Campaigns of Alexander,* trans. Aubrey de Sélincourt. New York: Penguin, 1971, pp. 278–79.

39. Warry, *Warfare,* p. 93.

Chapter 5: Oar, Sail, and Ram: Greek Warships and Their Crews

40. Thucydides, *The Peloponnesian War,* trans. Rex Warner. New York: Penguin, 1972, p. 37.

41. Thucydides, *Peloponnesian War,* p. 37.

42. Homer, *Odyssey,* trans. E.V. Rieu. Baltimore: Penguin, 1961, p. 94.

43. In the later years of the Peloponnesian War, when Athens found it increasingly difficult to find enough wealthy men of military age to take on this duty, the state resorted to having two men share it. In 340 B.C. the duty was spread further among several men. And in the late fourth century B.C., it was abolished altogether.

44. Xenophon, *Hellenica,* published as *A History of My Times,* trans. Rex Warner. New York: Penguin, 1979, p. 313.

45. Adcock, *Greek and Macedonian Art of War,* p. 38.

46. Lionel Casson, *The Ancient Mariners: Seafarers and Sea Fighters of the Mediterranean in Ancient Times.* Princeton: Princeton University Press, 1991, p. 101.

47. Aeschylus, *The Persians,* in *Prometheus Bound, The Suppliants, Seven Against Thebes, The Persians,* trans. Philip Vellacott. Baltimore: Penguin, 1961, p. 134.

48. Aeschylus, *Persians,* p. 134.

49. Diodorus Siculus, *Library of History,* in William L. Rodgers, *Greek and Roman Naval Warfare.* Annapolis, MD: Naval Institute Press, 1964, p. 241.

Chapter 6: The Cost of Disunity: Greek Armies Fall to Roman Steel

50. Hanson, *Wars of the Ancient Greeks,* p. 200.

51. Robert J. Littman, *The Greek Experiment: Imperialism and Social Conflict, 800–400 B.C.* London: Thames and Hudson, 1974, pp. 13–14, 20.

52. These cities, including Sybaris, Croton, Rhegium, and Tarentum, among many others, had been established in an intensive burst of Greek colonization spanning the period ca. 750–550 B.C. In Pyrrhus's day some were larger, and all were more cultured, than Rome.

53. Quoted in Plutarch, *Life of Pyrrhus,* in *Age of Alexander,* p. 399.

54. Quoted in Plutarch, *Life of Pyrrhus,* in *Age of Alexander,* p. 409.

55. Hanson, *Wars of the Ancient Greeks,* p. 198.

56. Polybius, *Histories,* p. 511.

57. Polybius, *Histories,* pp. 511–13.

58. Lawrence Keppie, *The Making of the Roman Army: From Republic to Empire.* New York: Barnes and Noble, 1984, p. 19.

59. Connolly, *Greece and Rome at War,* pp. 205–206.

60. Plutarch, *Life of Aemilius Paulus,* in *Lives of the Noble Grecians and Romans,* trans. John Dryden. New York: Random House, 1932, p. 333.

61. Quoted in Polybius, *Histories,* pp. 299–300.

Glossary

acropolis: "The city's high place"; a hill, usually fortified, central to many Greek towns; the term in uppercase (Acropolis) refers to the one in Athens.

agones: Contests.

antilabe: A leather handle on the back of a hoplite's shield that he gripped with his left hand.

bireme: An ancient ship having two banks of oars.

bronze: A metal alloy composed of copper and tin.

cuirass: A breastplate or other chest protection worn by an ancient infantryman.

diekplus: A Greek naval maneuver in which one group of ships attempted to sail through an enemy line, wheel around, and ram the opposing ships on their exposed backs and sides.

ekdromoi (singular is *ekdromos*): "Runners out"; light-armed hoplites who chased after peltasts.

en echelon: Obliquely; at an angle.

enomotiai (singular is *enomotia*): Twenty-five-man units within a phalanx.

epibatai: Hoplite marines who boarded enemy ships and fought hand-to-hand.

greaves: Bronze shin guards worn by Greek hoplites.

hetairoi: "Companion cavalry"; the principal cavalry unit in the army of Philip II and his son, Alexander the Great.

hippeis: Greek cavalry.

hoplite: A heavily armored infantry soldier.

hoplon (or *aspis*): The shield carried by a hoplite.

kubernetes: The helmsman on a Greek trireme, who was usually an experienced naval veteran.

legion: A large Roman military unit whose size varied over the centuries but that averaged about five thousand men.

linothorax: A cuirass made of layers of linen or canvas.

lochagos: The officer in command of a *lochos.*

lochos (plural is *lochoi*): A small subdivision of the Greek phalanx, composed of about a hundred men, though probably differing in size from one city-state to another.

maniple: A small Roman battlefield unit that usually consisted of either 60 or 120 men.

mercenary: A hired soldier.

mora (plural is *morai*): A large unit or battalion within the Spartan phalanx.

othismos: "The shoving"; a maneuver in which hoplites in the rear ranks of a phalanx pushed at their comrades' backs, forcefully thrusting the whole formation

95

into the enemy's ranks; if the enemy was Greek, its phalanx pushed back.

ouragoi: "Rear-rankers"; veteran officers who stood behind the phalanx and made sure the men in the rear ranks were doing their jobs.

paean: "Battle hymn"; a patriotic song sung by Greek hoplites as they marched into battle.

panoply: A hoplite's full array of arms and armor.

pelta: The small round or crescent-shaped shield carried by a peltast.

peltasts (*peltastai*): Light-armed skirmishers, usually javelin men.

pentekonter: A Greek ship with one bank of oars and fifty rowers.

pentekostyes: Fifty-man units within a phalanx.

periplus: A Greek naval maneuver in which one group of ships attempt to outflank (sail around the sides of) the enemy's vessels.

pezetairoi: "Foot-companions"; the name Macedonia's Philip II gave to the members of his phalanx.

phalanx: A Greek military formation consisting of multiple ranks, with hoplites standing, marching, or fighting side by side in each rank.

porpax: A bronze loop on the back of a hoplite's shield through which he placed his left arm.

psiloi: Poor citizens who sometimes accompanied Greek armies; they wore no armor and threw rocks.

pteruges: "Feathers"; strips of linen, canvas, or leather comprising the bottom part of a hoplite's linen cuirass.

quinquereme: A warship having three banks (levels) of oars, with two men to an oar in the top two banks and one man to an oar in the bottom bank.

sarissa: A long pike wielded by members of the Macedonian phalanx.

shield device: An emblem or other decoration on the outside of a shield.

strategos (plural is *strategoi*): In ancient Athens and some other Greek city-states, a military general, usually elected by a citizen-assembly.

taxis (plural is *taxeis*): A large subdivision of the Athenian phalanx, of which there were ten in all, each drawn from one of the city's tribes; the officer in command of a *taxis* was a *taxiarchos* (plural is *taxiarchoi*).

trierarch (*trierarchos*): The captain of a trireme; in Athens during the Classical Age, a trierarch assumed such command as part of a public duty known as the Trierarchy.

trireme (*trieres*): An ancient warship with three banks of oars, the *thranite* (upper), *zygite* (middle), and *thalamite* (lower).

trophy (*tropaion*): A wooden framework displaying captured enemy arms and armor; victors set one up on the battlefield to celebrate and give thanks to the gods.

For Further Reading

Isaac Asimov, *The Greeks: A Great Adventure.* Boston: Houghton Mifflin, 1965. An excellent, entertaining overview of Greek history and culture.

C.M. Bowra, *Classical Greece.* New York: Time-Life, 1965. Despite the passage of more than thirty years, this volume—written by a renowned classical historian and adorned with numerous maps, drawings, and color photos—is only slightly dated and remains one of the best introductions to ancient Greece for general readers.

Peter Connolly, *The Greek Armies.* Morristown, NJ: Silver Burdette, 1979. A fine, detailed study of Greek armor, weapons, and battle tactics, filled with colorful, accurate illustrations by Connolly, the world's leading artistic interpreter of the ancient world. Highly recommended.

———, *The Legend of Odysseus.* New York: Oxford University Press, 1986. An excellent, easy-to-read summary of the events of Homer's *Iliad* and *Odyssey,* including many informative sidebars about the way people lived in Mycenaean times. Also contains many stunning illustrations re-creating the fortresses, homes, ships, and armor of the period.

Denise Dersin, *Greece: Temples, Tombs, and Treasures.* Alexandria, VA: Time-Life, 1994. In a way a newer companion volume to Bowra's book (see above), this is also excellent and features a long, up-to-date, and beautifully illustrated chapter on Athens's golden age.

Will Fowler, *Ancient Weapons: The Story of Weaponry and Warfare Through the Ages.* New York: Lorenz Books, 1999. Beautifully illustrated with color drawings, this volume traces the history of various weapons used in ancient and medieval times, including those of the Greeks.

Susan Peach and Anne Millard, *The Greeks.* London: Usborne, 1990. A general overview of the history, culture, myths, everyday life, and warfare and weapons of ancient Greece, presented in a format suitable to young, basic readers (although the many fine, accurate color illustrations make the book appealing to anyone interested in ancient Greece).

Jonathon Rutland, *See Inside an Ancient Greek Town.* New York: Barnes and Noble, 1995. This colorful introduction to ancient Greek life is aimed at basic readers.

Author's Note: In the following volumes, I provide much useful background information about Greek history and culture, including the Greek-Persian conflict; the rise and fall of the Athenian empire; the golden age of arts, literature, and architecture; and sketches of the important Greek politicians, military leaders, writers, and artists. Though they are aimed at high school readers, the high level of detail and documentation in these volumes make them useful for older general readers as well.

Don Nardo, *The Age of Pericles.* San Diego: Lucent Books, 1996.

——, *Greek and Roman Sport.* San Diego: Lucent Books, 1999.

——, *Greek and Roman Theater.* San Diego: Lucent Books, 1995.

——, *Leaders of Ancient Greece.* San Diego: Lucent Books, 1999.

——, *Life in Ancient Athens.* San Diego: Lucent Books, 2000.

——, *The Parthenon.* San Diego: Lucent Books, 1999.

——, *Philip II and Alexander the Great Unify Greece.* Springfield, NJ: Enslow, 2000.

——, *The Trial of Socrates.* San Diego: Lucent Books, 1997.

Major Works Consulted

Modern Sources

F.E. Adcock, *The Greek and Macedonian Art of War.* Berkeley: University of California Press, 1957. An older but still very useful look at Greek warfare by a noted historian.

Lionel Casson, *The Ancient Mariners: Seafarers and Sea Fighters of the Mediterranean in Ancient Times.* Princeton: Princeton University Press, 1991. A reprint of Casson's classic 1959 book chronicling the evolution of ships, including warships and their crews, in the ancient Mediterranean. Highly recommended.

Peter Connolly, *Greece and Rome at War.* London: Greenhill Books, 1998. Lavishly illustrated by Connolly himself, this is a highly detailed synopsis of Greek and Roman arms, military uniforms, siege machines, warships, and much more. Highly recommended.

Robert Drews, *The End of the Bronze Age: Changes in Warfare and the Catastrophe ca. 1200 B.C.* Princeton: Princeton University Press, 1993. The best available general overview of Bronze Age warfare. Drews also summarizes the various theories for why the Mycenaean kingdoms collapsed and champions the idea that fighters from the periphery of the these realms found ways to overwhelm the Mycenaeans's chariot corps and other standard military elements.

Peter Green, *The Greco-Persian Wars.* Berkeley: University of California Press, 1996. A beautifully written, often riveting treatment of these pivotal conflicts that changed the fate of Europe forever.

P.A.L. Greenhalgh, *Early Greek Warfare: Horsemen and Chariots in the Homeric and Archaic Ages.* Cambridge: Cambridge University Press, 1973. Effectively summarizes present knowledge and scholarly debates about the uses of cavalry and chariots in early Greek warfare.

N.G.L. Hammond, *Philip of Macedon.* Baltimore: Johns Hopkins University Press, 1994. A fine overview of Philip's talents and exploits by one of the leading ancient military historians of the past century.

Victor D. Hanson, *The Wars of the Ancient Greeks and Their Invention of Western Military Culture.* London: Cassell, 1999. One of the better general synopses of Greek warfare for the general reader, this one heavily emphasizes the agrarian and social changes that, over time, altered the nature of Greek warfare and ultimately Western warfare in general.

———, *The Western Way of War: Infantry Battle in Classical Greece.* New York: Oxford University Press, 1989. An extremely well-written, well-documented overview of hoplite warfare by one of the world's leading experts in the field. Some of Hanson's descriptions of men in battle border on the poetic. Highly recommended to all.

John Lazenby, *The Defense of Greece.* Bloomington, IL: David Brown, 1993. Detailed and authoritative, this is one of the two best available scholarly works on the Greco-Persian conflicts. (The other is Peter Green's volume; see above.)

———, *The Spartan Army.* Warminster, England: Aris and Phillips, 1985. Lazenby here delivers another impressive volume on ancient military history, in this case a synopsis of the long-formidable Spartan army.

John D. Montagu, *Battles of the Greek and Roman Worlds.* London: Greenhill Books, 2000. A useful compendium of the major Greco-Roman battles, in each case briefly summarizing the background, setting, combatants, tactics, and results.

Nicholas Sekunda, *Warriors of Ancient Greece.* Oxford: Osprey, 1999. A short but information-packed overview of Greek military costumes and weapons during the Classical Age. Highly recommended to buffs of ancient military history.

Nicholas Sekunda and John Warry, *Alexander the Great: His Armies and Campaigns, 334–323 B.C.* London: Osprey, 1998. A useful, up-to-date short synopsis of Alexander's military organization and conquests written by two prominent ancient military historians.

A.M. Snodgrass, *Arms and Armour of the Greeks.* Baltimore: Johns Hopkins University Press, 1999. A reprint of the 1967 classic study of Greek weapons and warfare. Snodgrass, a noted expert in the field, provides some updated material in this version.

John Warry, *Warfare in the Classical World.* Norman: University of Oklahoma Press, 1995. A beautifully mounted book filled with accurate and useful paintings, drawings, maps, and diagrams. The text is also first rate, providing much detailed information about the weapons, clothing, strategies, battle tactics, and military leaders of the Greeks, Romans, and the peoples they fought.

Ancient Sources

Aeschylus, *The Persians,* in *Prometheus Bound, The Suppliants, Seven Against*

Thebes, The Persians. Trans. Philip Vellacott. Baltimore: Penguin, 1961.

Arrian, *Anabasis Alexandri,* published as *The Campaigns of Alexander.* Trans. Aubrey de Sélincourt. New York: Penguin, 1971.

Kenneth J. Atchity, ed., *The Classical Greek Reader.* New York: Oxford University Press, 1996.

Diodorus Siculus, *Library of History.* 12 vols. Trans. Charles L. Sherman and C. Bradford Welles. Cambridge, MA: Harvard University Press, 1963.

Herodotus, *The Histories.* Trans. Aubrey de Sélincourt. New York: Penguin, 1972.

Homer, *Odyssey.* Trans. E.V. Rieu. Baltimore: Penguin, 1961.

Plato, *Laws,* in *Great Books of the Western World.* Trans. Benjamin Jowett. Chicago: Encyclopaedia Britannica, 1952.

Plutarch, *Life of Aemilius Paulus* in Lives of the Noble Grecians and Romans, trans. John Dryden. New York: Randomhouse, 1932.

Plutarch, *Parallel Lives,* published complete as *Lives of the Noble Grecians and Romans.* Trans. John Dryden. New York: Random House, 1932; also,

excerpted in *The Rise and Fall of Athens: Nine Greek Lives by Plutarch.* Trans. Ian Scott-Kilvert. New York: Penguin, 1960; *The Age of Alexander: Nine Greek Lives by Plutarch.* Trans. Ian Scott-Kilvert. New York: Penguin, 1973; *Makers of Rome: Nine Lives By Plutarch.* Trans. Ian Scott-Kilvert. New York: Penguin, 1965.

Polybius, *Histories,* published as *Polybius: The Rise of the Roman Empire.* Trans. Ian Scott-Kilvert. New York: Penguin, 1979.

Thucydides, *The Peloponnesian War.* Trans. Rex Warner. New York: Penguin, 1972; also published as *The Landmark Thucydides: A Comprehensive Guide to the Peloponnesian War.* Ed. Robert B. Strassler. Trans. Richard Crawley. New York: Simon and Schuster, 1996.

Xenophon, *Anabasis.* Trans. W.H.D. Rouse. New York: New American Library, 1959.

———, *Hellenica,* published as *A History of My Times.* Trans. Rex Warner. New York: Penguin, 1979.

———, *Scripta Minora.* Trans. E.C. Marchant. Cambridge, MA: Harvard University Press, 1993.

Additional Works Consulted

Lesly Adkins and Roy A. Adkins, *Handbook to Life in Ancient Greece.* New York: Facts On File, 1997.

J.K. Anderson, *Military Theory and Practice in the Age of Xenophon.* Berkeley: University of California Press, 1970.

C.M. Bowra, *The Greek Experience.* New York: New American Library, 1957.

John Buckler, *The Theban Hegemony.* Cambridge, MA: Harvard University Press, 1980.

Andrew R. Burn, *Persia and the Greeks: The Defense of the West, c. 546–478 B.C.* London: Edward Arnold, 1962.

G.H. Chase, *The Shield Devices of the Greeks in Art and Literature.* Chicago: Ares, 1979. (A reprint of the original 1902 book.)

Oliver Dickinson, *The Aegean Bronze Age.* New York: Cambridge University Press, 1994.

Walter Donlon and James Thompson, "The Charge at Marathon," *Classical Journal,* vol. 71, 1976.

———, "The Charge at Marathon Again," *Classical Journal,* vol. 72, 1979.

Robert Drews, *The Coming of the Greeks: Indo-European Conquests in the Aegean and the Near East.* Princeton: Princeton University Press, 1988.

J.R. Ellis, *Philip II and Macedonian Imperialism.* New York: Thames and Hudson, 1977.

Donald W. Engels, *Alexander the Great and the Logistics of the Macedonian Army.* Berkeley: University of California Press, 1978.

Arther Ferrill, *The Origins of War.* New York: Westview Press, 1997.

M.I. Finley, *Early Greece: The Bronze and Archaic Ages.* New York: W. W. Norton, 1970.

J. Lesley Fitton, *Discovery of the Greek Bronze Age.* London: British Museum Press, 1995.

J.F.C. Fuller, *The Generalship of Alexander the Great.* New Brunswick, NJ: Rutgers University Press, 1960.

Robert Garland, *The Greek Way of Death.* Ithaca, NY: Cornell University Press, 1985.

Michael Grant, *The Classical Greeks.* New York: Scribner's, 1989.

———, *A Guide to the Ancient World.* New York: Barnes and Noble, 1996.

———, *The Rise of the Greeks.* New York: Macmillan, 1987.

G.T. Griffith, *Mercenaries of the Hellenistic World.* New York: AMS, 1977.

Erich Gruen, *The Hellenistic World and the Coming of Rome.* Berkeley: University of California Press, 1984.

Sir John Hackett, ed., *Warfare in the Ancient World.* New York: Facts On File, 1989.

Victor D. Hanson, *The Other Greeks: The Family Farm and the Agrarian Roots of Western Civilization.* New York: Simon and Schuster, 1995.

Donald Kagan, *The Outbreak of the Peloponnesian War.* Ithaca, NY: Cornell University Press, 1969.

Robert B. Kebric, *Greek People.* Mountain View, CA: Mayfield, 2001.

Lawrence Keppie, *The Making of the Roman Army: From Republic to Empire.* New York: Barnes and Noble, 1984.

Peter Levi, *Atlas of the Greek World.* New York: Facts On File, 1984.

Robert J. Littman, *The Greek Experiment: Imperialism and Social Conflict,* *800–400 B.C.* London: Thames and Hudson, 1974.

Nanno Marinatos, *Art and Religion in Thera: Reconstructing a Bronze Age Society.* Athens, Greece: D. and I. Mathioulakis, 1984.

Thomas R. Martin, *Ancient Greece: From Prehistoric to Hellenistic Times.* New Haven, CT: Yale University Press, 1996.

Malcolm F. McGregor, *The Athenians and Their Empire.* Vancouver: University of British Columbia Press, 1987.

Christian Meier, *Athens: Portrait of a City in Its Golden Age.* Trans. Robert and Rita Kimber. New York: Henry Holt, 1998.

A.J. Podlecki, *The Life of Themistocles.* Montreal: McGill-Queen's University Press, 1975.

William L. Rodgers, *Greek and Roman Naval Warfare.* Annapolis, MD: Naval Institute Press, 1964.

H.H. Scullard, *The Elephant in the Greek and Roman World.* Ithaca, NY: Cornell University Press, 1974.

Chester G. Starr, *A History of the Ancient World.* New York: Oxford University Press, 1991.

L.J. Worley, *Hippeis: The Cavalry of Ancient Greece.* Boulder, CO: Westview Press, 1994.

Index

Picture Credits

About the Author

Historian Don Nardo has written numerous volumes about the ancient Greek world, including *The Age of Pericles, Greek and Roman Sport, The Parthenon, Life in Ancient Athens,* and *The Greenhaven Encyclopedia of Greek and Roman Mythology.* He is also the editor of Greenhaven's *Complete History of Ancient Greece* and literary companions to the works of Homer and Sophocles. Along with his wife, Christine, he resides in Massachusetts.